# THE FACTORY OF THE FUTURE

SOCIO-TECHNICAL
INVESTMENT
MANAGEMENT

EUROPEAN
METHODS

DOCUMENT OFFICIELS

APR 1 1992

GOVERNMENT
PUBLICATIONS

# THE FACTORY OF THE FUTURE

## SOCIO-TECHNICAL INVESTMENT MANAGEMENT

## EUROPEAN METHODS

**Olivier du ROY (AEGIST)**

Final report of the working party established by the European Foundation for the Improvement of Living and Working Conditions — 1990

European Foundation
for the Improvement of
Living and Working Conditions

**Text:**
Olivier du Roy (AEGIST)
Pascal Paoli (co-ordinator and Research Manager, European Foundation for Improvement of Living and Working Conditions)
Original language: French
Translated by: Cave Translations Ltd, UK

**Production:**
Foundation's Publications Officer: Susan Ryan-Sheridan
Design and typesetting: Printset & Design Ltd., Dublin
Printing: Criterion Press Ltd.

Luxembourg: Office for Official Publications of the European Communities, 1992

ISBN 92-826-3529-5

Catalogue number: SY-72-91-980-EN-C

©Copyright: European Foundation for the Improvement of Living and Working Conditions, 1992. For rights of translation or reproduction, applications should be made to the Director, European Foundation for the Improvement of Living and Working Conditions, Loughlinstown House, Shankill, Co. Dublin, Ireland

# Preface

Economic performance and the quality of the working environment are inextricably intertwined, which is why social and economic aspects must be reconciled. It is no longer acceptable for social factors to be treated as the adjustment variable when technical and financial decisions are being made.

In the context of heightened international competition, the optimization of investment has become a condition of survival. There is no longer any margin for error, which means that social and technical issues must be considered simultaneously. Right from the very beginning of an investment project, it is essential that careful thought be given to organizational choices, occupational skills, ergonomics and plant management.

The question is how to proceed, how to reverse the logic according to which most enterprises give priority to technical issues and the last word to the engineer? This is the question we shall attempt to answer in this report by outlining a possible methodology and drawing some examples from the approaches taken by a number of enterprises in the European Community.

Of course, socio-technical integration is not something that can merely be decreed. The methods suggested here depend to a certain extent on an enterprise culture that allows a good deal of room for participation and negotiation. This implies a change not only in procedures but also in habits and attitudes, a reviewing of everyone's role, from the manager to the trade-union representative. The Foundation hopes that this report will contribute to the development of a European approach to the management of change.

Clive Purkiss  
Director

Eric Verborgh  
Deputy Director

# Contents

| | | |
|---|---|---|
| **Introduction** | | 9 |
| **Part One** | Joint design or socio-technical design | 15 |
| **Part Two** | From social system to socio-organizational system: the enrichment of technical projects | 23 |
| **Part Three** | Time management: the key factor in a socio-technical project | 31 |
| **Part Four** | The design team: the various roles in the management of a project | 41 |
| **Part Five** | User participation | 47 |
| **Part Six** | The role of workers' representatives and trade-union organizations | 53 |
| **Part Seven** | Studies of existing situations as "reference situations" | 65 |
| **Part Eight** | Socio-technical specifications | 73 |
| **Part Nine** | Identifying alternatives | 81 |
| **Part Ten** | The organization at the design stage | 89 |
| **Part Eleven** | The integration of forward management of work and training in the design process | 97 |
| **Part Twelve** | The financial viability of a socio-technical approach to investment | 105 |
| **Part Thirteen** | Project evaluation | 115 |
| **Conclusion** | | 121 |
| **Bibliography** | | 125 |

This report, drawn up and edited by Olivier du Roy, is the result of the studies of a working party organized and co-ordinated by Pascal Paoli of the European Foundation for the Improvement of Living and Working Conditions.

The members of the working party, which met five times in 1988 and 1989, were:

**Jacques T ALLEGRO**
Nederlands Instituut voor Arbeidsomstandigheden (NIA), Netherlands

**Lars Erik ANDREASEN**
Commission of the European Communities, Belgium

**Emilio Castejon VILELLA**
Instituto Nacional de Seguridad e Higiene en el Trabajo, Spain

**Xénofon CONSTANTIDINIS**
Société Aluminium de Grèce, Greece

**Olivier du ROY and Stany REGOUT**
AEGIST, Belgium

**Werner FRICKE**
Friedrich-Ebert Stiftung, Federal Republic of Germany

**Jean-Baptiste HERVE and Robert VILLATTE**
Institut pour l'Amélioration des Conditions de Travail (INPACT), France

**Denis REGNAUD**
CISTE, France

**Pierre-Louis REMY**
ANACT, France

**Matteo ROLLIER**
RSO, Italy

**Peter SCHUH**
IQUI, Federal Republic of Germany

**Reginald SELL**
Work Research Unit, United Kingdom

**Ray WILD**
The Management College, Henley, United Kingdom

# THE FACTORY OF THE FUTURE
SOCIO-TECHNICAL INVESTMENT MANAGEMENT
— EUROPEAN METHODS

# INTRODUCTION

## The socio-technical approach: an old subject with a new twist

The socio-technical approach to investment management emerged in the 1970s as a result of the wish to take account of working conditions, health and safety at work and job enrichment ("de-Taylorization") in technical projects. It was the opinion of enterprises, consultants, social scientists and ergonomists that these issues should be tackled at an earlier stage than was then the norm, perhaps even when plants or factories were being designed.

Some major experiments, particularly in Scandinavian countries, illustrated the possibilities of radical innovation and of finding alternatives to assembly-line work.

The issue has re-emerged since the early 1980s, but this time with a new twist, the emphasis now being on economic rather than social factors. Modern production management based on new computer-aided technologies and the changes and technical innovations that have affected every industrial sector have revealed an urgent need for new methods of organization. It has become apparent that appropriate management and labour structures need to be established long before new plants are set up.

## The central issue: investment management

Some industrial groups and management consultants then suggested that the central problem was investment management itself: the Taylorism of the finished product was merely the fruit of a Taylorist approach in which the end-user had no say in the design of his tools.

This is the conclusion reached after 15 years of research in this field and is the key issue discussed in this report, in which we shall present the fundamental concepts underlying all methods of socio-technical project management (socio-technical joint design).

The aim of these methods or approaches is the *joint* definition or design of technical investment and human organization in industrial projects. These methods are also applied in the design of data-processing and office systems, but we shall concentrate here on industrial projects.

The basis of these methods is the desire to deal with organizational or social problems, not after the event, but at the very time that technical changes or new plants offer the opportunity of joint redefinition, together with wider margins for manoeuvre: the ideal situation is that of the "greenfield plant".

## Participation: just one factor

The key issue is not so much the participation of the personnel involved or of their representative bodies (as it is in the case of other research projects undertaken by the Foundation), but rather a joint multidisciplinary approach to industrial design, in which social, organizational, technical and economic factors are all taken into account.

Participation and negotiation undoubtedly have a role to play here and most practitioners and theorists in this field see them as essential ingredients of good joint design. They are also vital prerequisites if the work-force is successfully to adapt to new technologies. This is why participation and negotiation are included among the methodological concepts discussed later in this report.

## Key concepts in socio-technical project management

Our intention is to focus our report on some *key concepts* in the socio-technical approach to industrial design. We shall not be covering all the concepts underlying that approach, but shall merely give some pointers as to how the theory can be put into practice in a *design process* when a workshop, production line or, better still, a factory is being built from scratch.

Nor do we intend to give a detailed description of the methods used, with their complicated configuration of successive stages, because it would seem that these "methodological configurations" are very dependent on national context and on the type of industry or sector involved.

It therefore seemed preferable to present concepts separately — concepts that constantly recur, to varying degrees and with different emphases, whatever the method used. Their presence may be a constant, but the chronological order in which they arise can vary considerably.

These concepts are (in the order in which they are to be discussed):

- joint design or socio-technical design;
- from "social system" to socio-organizational system: the enrichment of technical projects;
- time management: the key factor in a socio-technical project;
- the design team and the various roles in the management of a project;
- user participation;
- the role of workers' representatives and trade-union organizations;
- studies of existing situations as "reference situations";
- socio-technical specifications;

- identifying alternatives;
- the organization at the design stage;
- the integration of forward management of work and training in the design process;
- the financial viability of a socio-technical approach to investment;
- project evaluation as a source of progress.

## The purpose of this report

This report is published under the aegis of the European Foundation for the Improvement of Living and Working Conditions in Dublin and is the result of numerous meetings with experts, enterprises and trade-unionists in the major EEC countries. It has three aims:

☐ *to make all the industrial partners aware* of innovative methods of investment management which are particularly appropriate in a context of rapid industrial modernization, in which everyone agrees that *the preparation of the human factor and the modernization of organizations are as important as technical change*;

☐ *to contribute to social dialogue and negotiation* by indicating new methods and alternatives to the traditional approach. Where, in the past, *the social impact of technical decisions* was discussed only after the event, it is now being discussed before, or as, issues arise. This implies that the two sides of industry are prepared to take a socio-economic approach;

☐ *to review existing methods.* This report should give both industrial enterprises and trade unions an idea of the various methods currently being used and enable them to gain an understanding of their underlying principles and implications. The aim is to give a broad overview, picking out major concepts.

# THE FACTORY OF THE FUTURE
SOCIO-TECHNICAL INVESTMENT MANAGEMENT — EUROPEAN METHODS

# PART ONE

# JOINT DESIGN
or socio-technical design

Joint design is the term coined in the USA by L E Davis to describe the joint design of social and technical systems. Davis's idea was to establish joint design as an alternative and a challenge to the dominance or sovereignty of technical design which refuses, or forgets, to take account of the question of "how technology will be used". The question is unavoidable and an engineer who refuses to tackle it is merely being naïve and revealing all his unconscious assumptions about the human functioning of industrial organizations.

The technical system and the social system (characteristics of the work-force from the point of view of age, sex, education and training, occupational culture, expectations, etc) must be *considered jointly*. The meeting point of these two systems is the *organization*, as illustrated in the diagram, which will be discussed on several occasions in this report. See Figure 1 below:

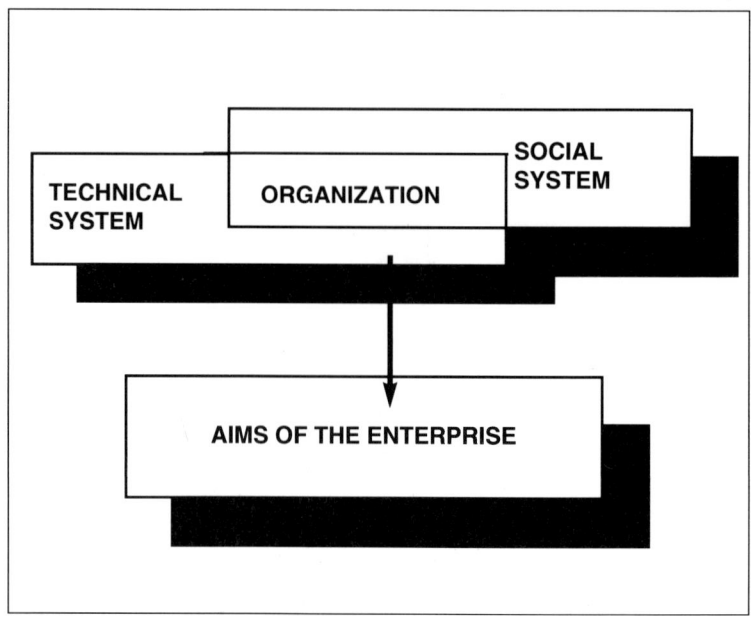

**FIGURE 1**

## The socio-organizational system is not merely a consequence, it is an *input datum*

The first requirement of socio-technical design is that the socio-organizational system must be seen as being *as important* and decisive as the technical system. It is not merely *an effect* caused by a given technical system, manipulated to use that system as effectively as possible; it is an "input datum", a source of constraints that must be taken into account or accepted.

## Social design and technical design must be *simultaneous*

Yet this means that "joint design" is also "simultaneous design" and that social constraints or organizational projects must be defined *at the same time as*, ie *simultaneously* with, the technical system, and not afterwards, as is often the case in traditional design.

## Design must be *interactive*

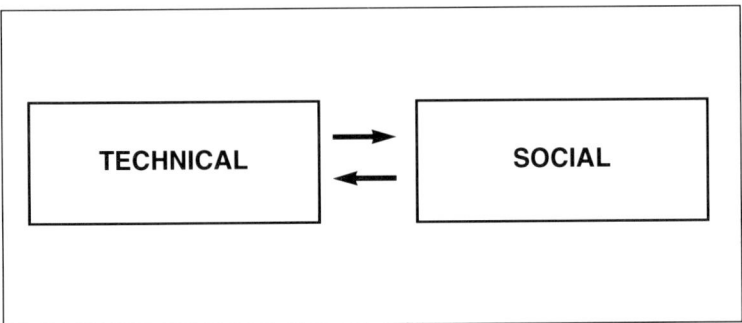

**FIGURE 2**

Finally, joint design is also *interactive design* (and therefore often repetitive), with interaction between the socio-organizational and technical aspects. This means that there must be "play", give and take, dialogue. To achieve this, as we say elsewhere, it is essential to create *alternatives* and to ensure that the project includes dialogue between several actors and several types of expertise.

We shall now give two examples of issues raised by the organizational system that must be responded to by the technical system, and of challenges posed by the technical system to the organizational system; these examples illustrate how important it is to see technical and organizational systems as being interactive.

## Example 1

An *enterprise manufacturing glass for use in vehicles* wants to build a new, highly automated factory. Its organizational plan aims to integrate its concern for quality in the actual design of its production lines, because *quality is to be assured* by production workers rather than by quality controllers.

Joint design in this case consists of looking at each point of the production line when the technical system is being designed, of identifying those points at which the quality of the product can be checked and how the information thus gathered can be used either to stimulate automatic backtracking or to indicate to operators the corrections that need to be made to the production process. If quality is to be taken into account *during the manufacturing process*, this information must also be fed to those who can make the necessary corrections, at the point where they can take action.

It is clear in this case that the manufacturer's concern for quality means that the design of the production system must make it possible for him to monitor quality *during the manufacturing process*, not once that process has been completed. This is an ideal example of a case in which an organizational factor has an impact on the design of the technical system.

## Example 2

A *paper-manufacturing enterprise* is modernizing a continuous-production machine by having it controlled by a process computer. From now on, most settings will be automated: the regulator connections are such that the machine has become a single system from beginning to end.

In the past, the entire organization of work and occupations rested on the fact that each operator was a specialist in one of the processes now performed by the machine: refining, wet end (forming the sheet), drying, sizing, etc. The technical transformation of the production process obviously means that the enterprise will have to rethink its entire organization for operating the machine, including skill systems.

We can see here how a technical change cannot be effectively introduced without reconsideration of both the social and organizational systems.

## Joint design: an approach faced by dual constraints

Finally, whatever the interplay between the technical and social systems, what counts is that the designer of a coherent social and technical system is faced by two types of constraints and aims from two different sources;

THE FACTORY OF THE FUTURE

this implies *a balanced review*, as is clearly illustrated by Renault's method.

This method stipulates that any socio-technical presentation of a project must clearly demonstrate the balance and interplay between technical and operational choices.

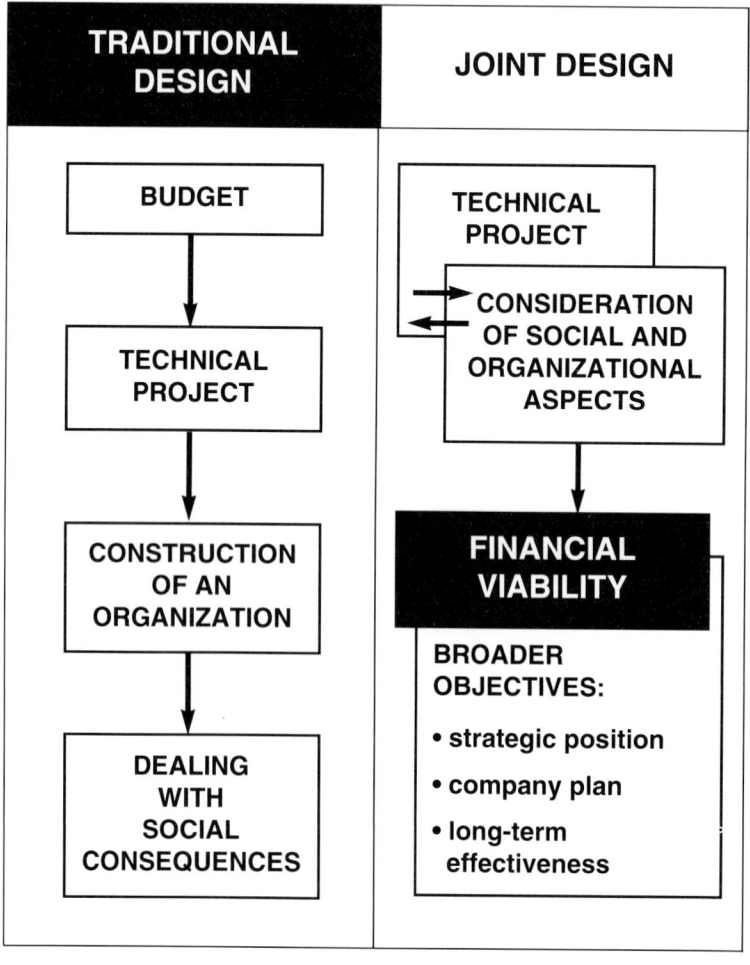

**FIGURE 3**

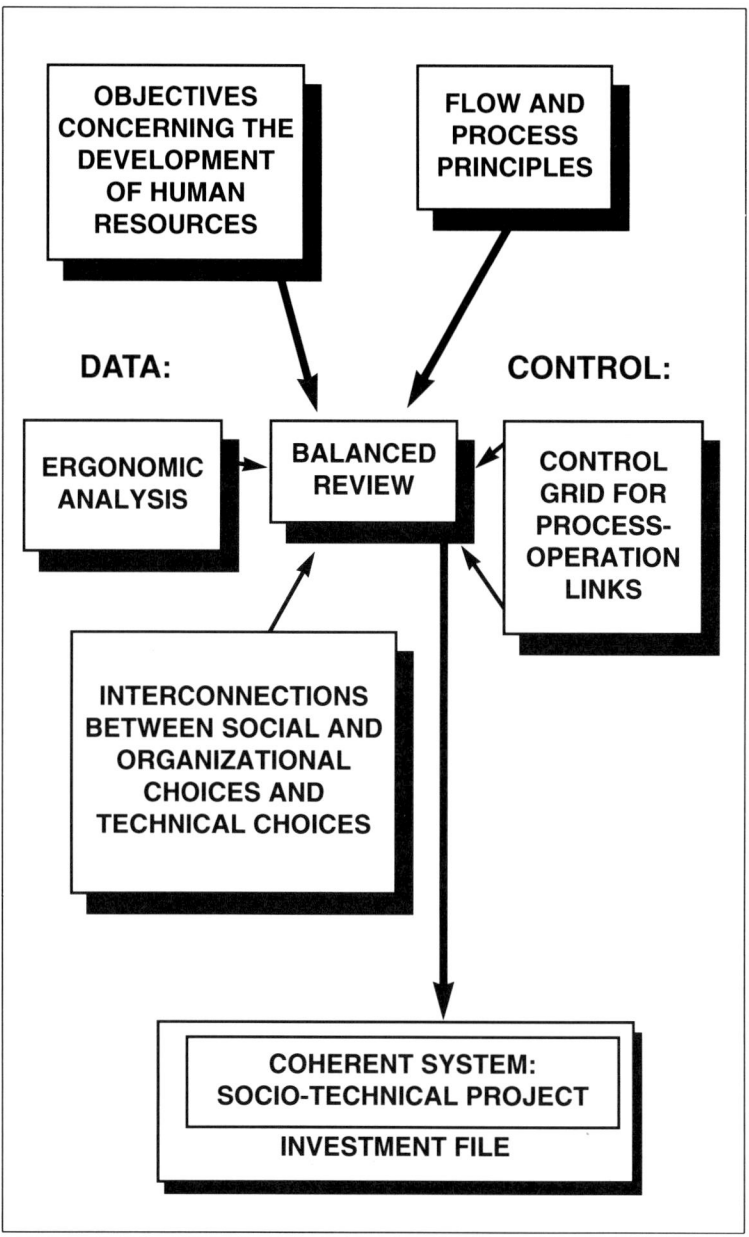

FIGURE 4

# THE FACTORY OF THE FUTURE

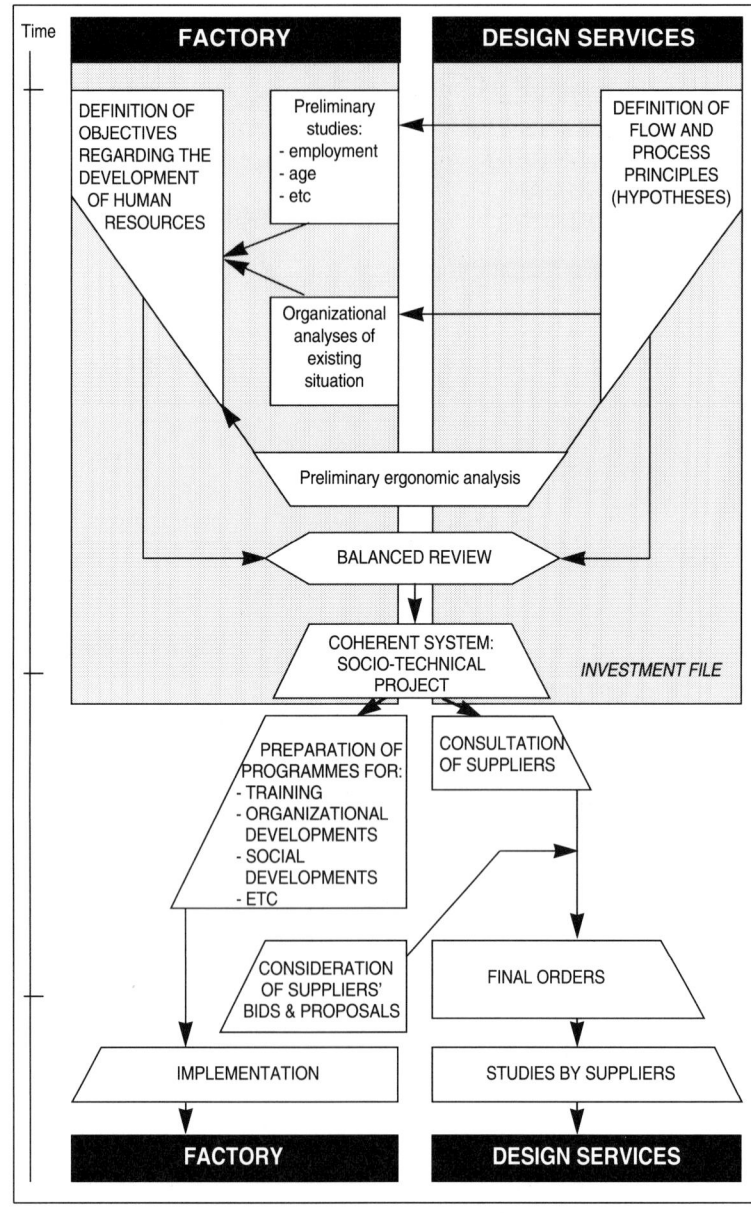

**FIGURE 5**  TOWARDS A SOCIO-TECHNICAL APPROACH TO PRODUCTION TECHNOLOGY (Fréd. Decoster, ANACT, March 1989)

# THE FACTORY OF THE FUTURE
SOCIO-TECHNICAL INVESTMENT MANAGEMENT — EUROPEAN METHODS

# PART TWO

# FROM SOCIAL SYSTEM TO SOCIO-ORGANIZATIONAL SYSTEM:
the enrichment of technical projects

## The social system, in the broadest sense

The "social" aspect of a socio-technical system should be understood to mean the entire socio-organizational system, including work-force skill structures. Everything to do with work and employment forms part of the social system.

Many methods were developed in the 1970s to integrate health and safety and working conditions in the design of plant and equipment, and these methods and their theoretical contributions are still of fundamental importance. They are very often the point of departure for methodological considerations of the "socio-technical management of industrial projects".

During the 1980s, however, the issue became much broader:

- ☐ firstly, as a result of consideration of the *organization of work* and the resulting *skill structures*;

- ☐ secondly, because of the *development of information and management systems*, which began to play an increasingly decisive role in the functioning of industrial plants;

- ☐ and finally, as a result of consideration of the full range of *operational problems*, including functional and organizational problems, as seen by the *operator* or *user*. This also covers, in part, what socio-technical analysis of the 1970s referred to as the analysis of "variables" or contingent factors.

## The enrichment of technical projects

The concept of the enrichment of objectives or technical projects was introduced by du Roy and Tubiana in France and was first tested in the BSN group.[1] Referred to as "project enrichment", the concept is a transference of a similar concept used in the 1960s and 70s, after Herzberg: "job enrichment".

Industrial projects are *at the outset* "poor", ie purely technical. To broaden their scope and "recharge" them by taking account of other parameters (working conditions, health and safety, organization, practical use, longer-term outlook, etc), authors proposed the introduction of the concept and method of enrichment at various stages of the project:

> ☐ *Enriching a project consists first and foremost of broadening its scope and increasing its objectives* so that it looks beyond the "hard technical core of the project". It is, then, in a sense, a *reframing* of the project. This is why some authors have proposed the use of a systematic investigation grid, based on *four axes of enrichment*. See Figure 6.

These four axes can be used to enrich a project, either on the basis of *known problems in former situations* (called "reference situations") or by *anticipating the consequences* of the investment (see later section on the anticipation of future work).

But they may also be used to *update an enterprise's policies or objectives* in general, which is why a project can be enriched by consideration of three areas:

> ☐ known *PROBLEMS* that the project provides an opportunity to solve;
>
> ☐ the anticipated *CONSEQUENCES* of technical change;
>
> ☐ the *POLICIES* followed with regard to the investment.

## AXES OF ENRICHMENT

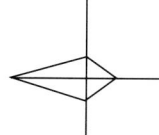

1. Anticipate future functioning, ie examine the conditions of use of the investment

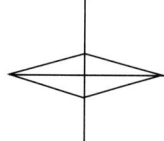

2. Analyse more carefully the possible impact on the work-force, working conditions and skill structures

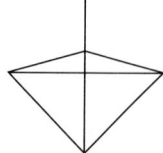

3. Consider the viewpoints of all the actors, ie reconsider the issue of organization and social relations

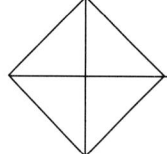

4. Look further (development of techniques, products, supplies, work-force) to put the technical changes involved in perspective and anticipate future developments

**FIGURE 6**

# FROM SOCIAL SYSTEM TO SOCIO-ORGANIZATIONAL SYSTEM

## TOOL: "THE FOUR AXES"

| AXES OF ENRICHMENT | PARAMETERS TO BE STUDIED | Is there a problem in the current situation? | Could there be a problem regarding future equipment? | The investment could resolve it! |
|---|---|---|---|---|
| OPERATING CONDITIONS | 1. Quality<br>2. Period of use of equipment<br>3. Flexibility<br>4. Work-force productivity<br>5. Materials and energy productivity<br>6. Maintenance conditions | | | |
| WORKING CONDITIONS | 7. Health and safety, social facilities<br>8. Physical environment<br>9. Workload<br>10. Job content and job satisfaction<br>11. Communication and co-operation<br>12. Advancement and training | | | |
| LABOUR RELATIONS AND ORGANIZATION | 13. Work-force structure and skills<br>14. Hierarchy and organization chart<br>15. Information and production-management system<br>16. Links with upstream and downstream activities, and with departments<br>17. Flows, traffic, stocks<br>18. Links with the environment | | | |
| DEVELOPMENTS | 19. Development of the factory<br>20. Development of technology<br>21. Development of the work-force and of the environment<br>22. Development of products, raw materials and energy<br>23. Development of legislation<br>24. Development of industrial relations | | | |

**FIGURE 7**

# THE FACTORY OF THE FUTURE

To enrich a project is also to pay special attention to the *areas of interface between the social* and technical systems; if care is not taken, the technical system tends to be defined with the narrow outlook of the technician.

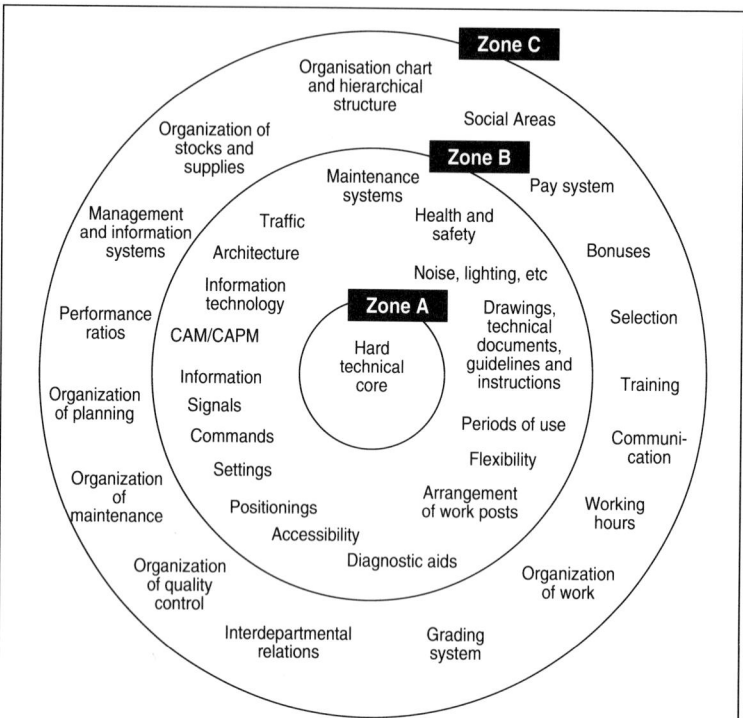

It is usual for Zones A and C to be dealt with separately in an industrial project. Some people are responsible for the technical core of the project, while others, at a later stage and when the technical project has been largely fixed, are responsible for considering organization, personnel issues and training. Consequently Zone B is dealt with from a purely technical viewpoint, and not as a meeting point of technical objectives and social and organizational considerations. Yet it is on Zone B that the coherence, and often the success, of the project depends.

This intermediate zone (Zone B) is the user's area of expertise. If the objectives of a project are to be enriched, it is important that, at a very early stage, this zone benefits from:

1. an analysis of the existing situation, former investment projects and users' experience;
2. an organizational project that can still modify if not the hard core at least the interface zone.

**FIGURE 8**

Project enrichment therefore comes into play at *every stage of a project* and bears on every aspect of that project:

- □ *enrichment of objectives:* it is when the fundamental constraints of the project are being defined that objectives must be enriched. Hence the idea of a project with multiple objectives: social, financial, technical, etc;

- □ *enrichment of research* is therefore a vital ingredient: if objectives and, later, specifications and solutions are to be enriched, it is essential that a number of studies be conducted on how the enterprise functions or of analogous situations or "reference situations";

- □ this necessarily leads to the *enrichment of specifications* when invitations to tender are being sent to suppliers: enriched technical specifications are specifications that lay down constraints other than those relating purely to technical performance — constraints concerning quality, working conditions, health and safety, impact on the skill structure of the work-force, etc;

- □ even *calculation of the financial viability of the investment* can be *enriched* by ensuring that it takes account of hidden costs (and hidden benefits) which are not usually considered by the enterprise's management systems;

- □ and finally, *the project itself is enriched* in a more general sense, in that the project blueprint is made more complex, involving more actors and being enriched primarily by the involvement of users (production, personnel-management, maintenance and quality-control staff), experts (ergonomists, sociologists, organization specialists, etc) and workers and their representatives.

---

REFERENCES

1. O du Roy *et al*, "Réussir l'investissement productif" (Successful investment in production), Editions d'Organisation, 1985

# THE FACTORY OF THE FUTURE
SOCIO-TECHNICAL INVESTMENT MANAGEMENT — EUROPEAN METHODS

## PART THREE

## TIME MANAGEMENT: THE KEY FACTOR IN A SOCIO-TECHNICAL PROJECT

THE FACTORY OF THE FUTURE

Time management is one of the vital ingredients of socio-technical project management, primarily because the meeting of deadlines and the clear definition of the various stages are a fundamental constraint of any investment project.

The importance of time management can be illustrated in three ways. See Figure 9 below:

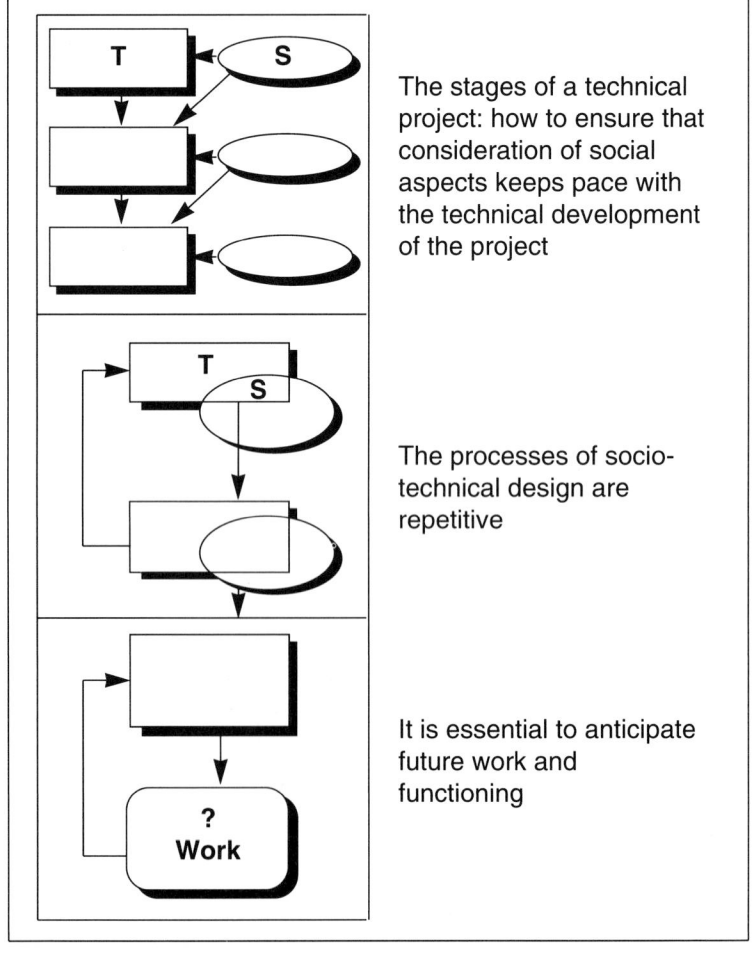

**FIGURE 9**

## Social issues involved in technical phases

Some people insist on the need to *"stick to"* engineering phases so that socio-organizational aspects are not taken into account too late. They are influenced by the inexorable nature of the unfolding over time of the major industrial projects in which they have taken part. Hence the concern of some methods (particularly French ones) rigorously to identify the social issues at stake in each phase of a project (preliminary studies, pilot study, project, implementation, start-up, etc), with particular emphasis on points of no return.

It is important that consideration of the human system and organizational aspects *does not* lag behind as the technical project advances. This means that the project must be organized in such a way that it *brings together all the different concerns* and departments of the enterprise (as will be discussed in Part Four), but also that these aspects must be fully integrated in the PERT (programme evaluation and review technique) of the project.

### Example

**A factory for the manufacture of foodstuffs** is being built in France. The enterprise wishes simultaneously to increase the productivity of its work-force, achieve better synchronization of the flow of products off the production line with weighing and packing operations, and improve working conditions. A study of work organization on similar production lines in two other factories points to the need to design production lines around a central control point from which the team can:

☐ monitor the packing process;

☐ conduct some more detailed checks;

# THE FACTORY OF THE FUTURE

☐ be ready to deal with situations requiring action by the entire team;

☐ manage the line's production.

The layout and architectural design of the factory have, however, already been fixed, which means that it is no longer possible to change the arrangement of production lines.

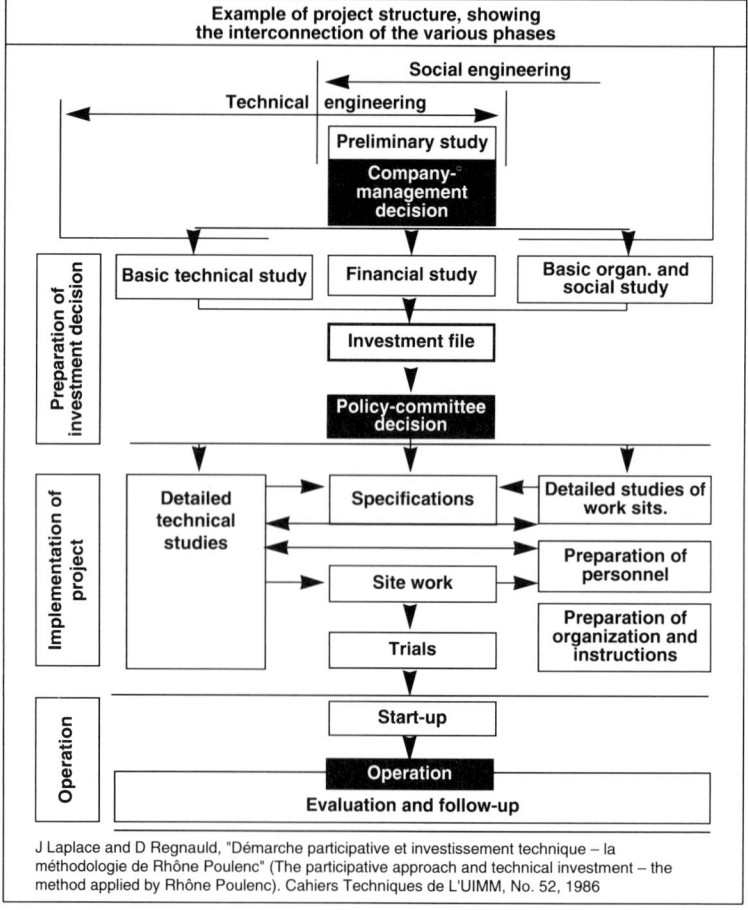

J Laplace and D Regnauld, "Démarche participative et investissement technique – la méthodologie de Rhône Poulenc" (The participative approach and technical investment – the method applied by Rhône Poulenc). Cahiers Techniques de L'UIMM, No. 52, 1986

**FIGURE 10**

## Towards a repetitive design

*Other people* rightly stress the necessarily *repetitive* nature of design processes.

The organization and the system can be optimized only if there is constant toing and froing, constant consideration, stage by stage, of the need to ensure that work on the organizational system and work on the technical system are progressing in unison.

This leads to the introduction, where possible (ie in some progressive projects), of the notion of experimenting, of *trying things out*, before re-examining ideas and applying them at a more general level.

Another example of this method of *repetition* is when past investments are systematically assessed with a view to improving and correcting the targeting of the next project.

Figure 11 shows a methodological framework devised by L E Davis:

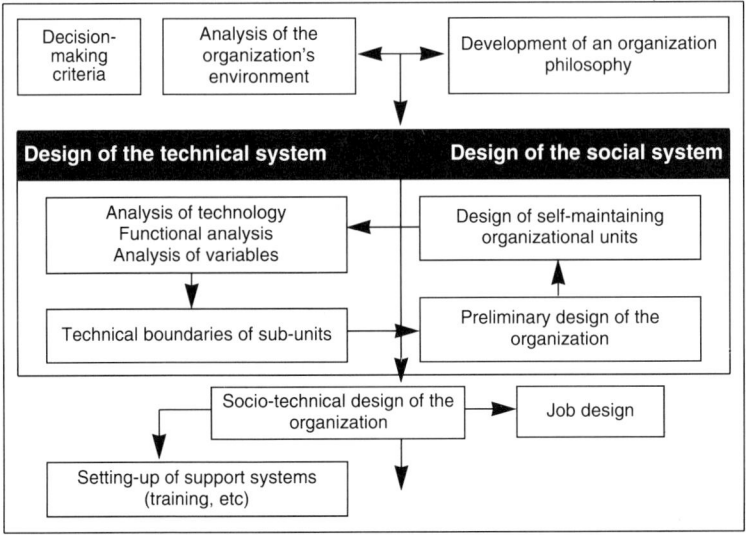

**FIGURE 11**

## Another example of an approach based on a repetitive process

Taken from "Sozialverträgliche Gestaltung von Automatisierungsvorhaben" (Shaping automation projects via social compacts), VDI, February 1989, p 12

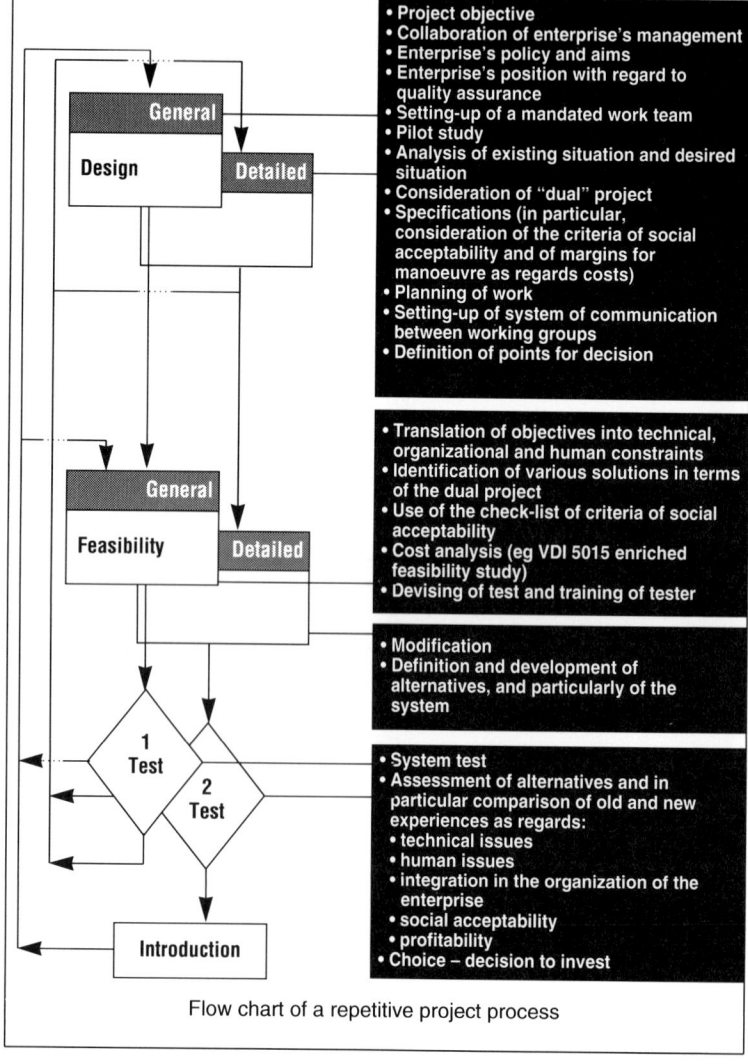

Flow chart of a repetitive project process

**FIGURE 12**

## Anticipation of future work and functioning

Finally, a *third approach* to time management is a fundamental element of joint design: *anticipation*. The challenge faced by joint design is that of *constantly anticipating* the effects of the planned technical systems so as to identify (at the design stage) any adjustments that need to be made and to establish repetition as part of the design process.

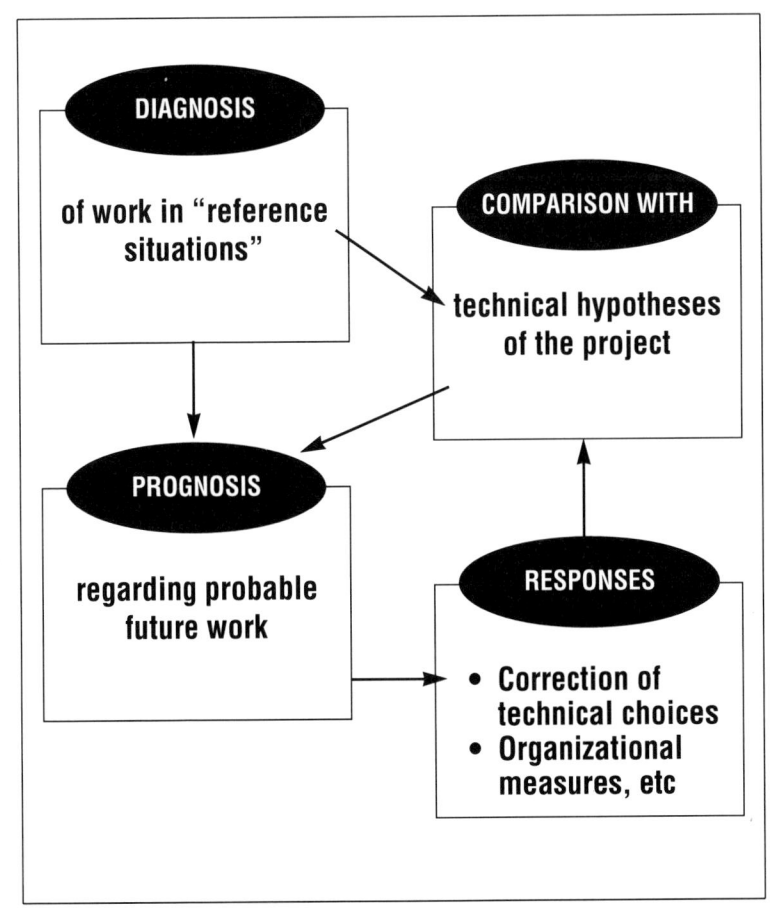

**FIGURE 13**

F Daniéllou has conferred scientific status on an empirical methodology we developed in 1979-80. At the time, we called it "anticipation of future work", or "prognosis" as opposed to "diagnosis" based on the current situation and "reference situations".

To quote Daniéllou:

> "Forecast reconstructions of probable future activity (...) lead to a prognosis bearing on this point. Signs of faulty adaptation can be identified; we are dealing here with characteristics of work resources which constrain activity in a manner incompatible with health or performance.
>
> The interaction between these 'reconstructions' and the design process is of a repetitive nature; any signs of faulty adaptation which are found give rise to fresh studies (technical, organizational, etc); new solutions can be proposed, which can again be subjected to the test of 'forecasting' future activity..."

Daniéllou[1] lays down three essential conditions for these "anticipations":

☐ the future operators must be present;

☐ there must be a prefiguration of future work resources (models, layouts, simulators, etc);

☐ an analysis must be made of typical situations (start-up, tool changes, settings, running repairs, various incidents, etc).

In 1985, we wrote in "Réussir l'investissement productif" (Successful investment in production), p 76:

> "What has to be achieved here is a *simulation of functioning* (...) This capacity for simulation

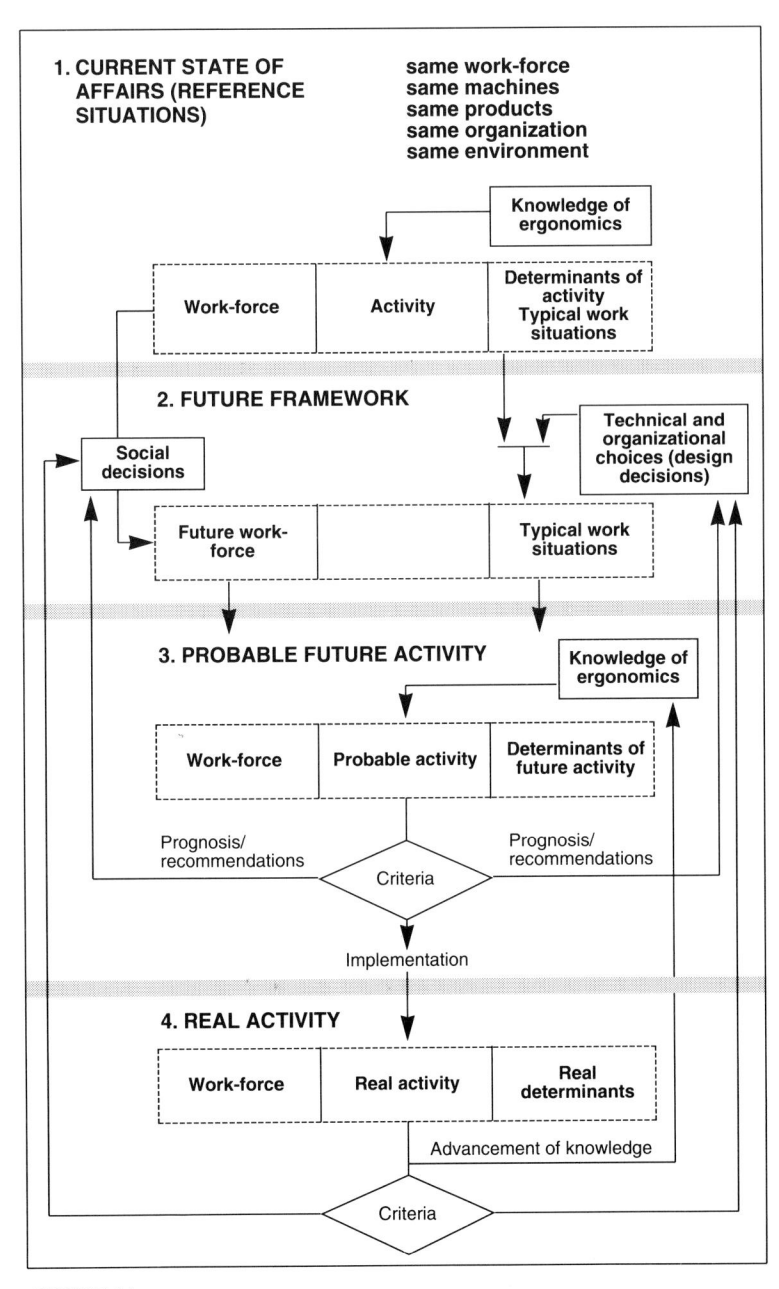

**FIGURE 14**

is one of the most characteristic aptitudes of operational personnel. That is why, by involving them in an investment project, one is assured of removing the maximum number of potential problems."

---

REFERENCES

1. See F Daniéllou, "Ergonomie et projets industriels" (Ergonomics and industrial projects), CNAM, Paris, 1988-89, pp 12-1 to 12-9. See also Figure 14 on p 39, which is taken from the same publication, p 4-2.

   See also F Daniéllou and A Garrigou, "Analyse du travail et conception des situations de travail" (Analysis of work and the design of work situations), in "Analyses du travail, enjeux et formes", CEREQ, Collection des Etudes, No. 54, March 1990, pp 79-84, and, by the same authors, "La mise en oeuvre des représentations des situations passées et des situations futures dans la participation des opérateurs à la conception" (Using representations of past and future situations in workers' participation in design), CNAM seminar, "Représentation pour l'action".

# The Factory of the Future
## Socio-technical Investment Management — European Methods

## Part Four

## The Design Team: The Various Roles in the Management of a Project

The socio-technical method of managing investments rests to a large extent on selection of the blueprint for project management, on the division of roles and on the constitution of the teams responsible for conducting the project.

- ☐ The central core of this blueprint is the establishment of a *project team* representing several points of view and multidisciplinary skills. "Several points of view" means those of the various functions of the enterprise; "multidisciplinary skills" means those of technical experts, specialists in information technology, management systems, organization and social sciences.

- ☐ Particular emphasis is placed on the choice and mandate of the *project leader:* his responsibilities must be clearly identified; he must be a good chairman, capable of guiding open debate in a multidisciplinary team whose members represent several different points of view, some of them contradictory; and he must be decisive and capable of respecting agreed deadlines and cost-limits. In brief, the project leader must be a real all-round manager.

- ☐ The tendency of the French "school" is to set up a *manufacturer's project group to balance the technical designer's project team:* this group is then responsible for representing the contracting enterprise (particularly as regards its interests as user and future manager of the investment) in relations with the engineering firm or research office, as well as in relations with the various suppliers of studies or technologies, whether internal or external. This approach has probably been adopted because it is the best way of dealing with major projects, which are largely externalized in that they are entrusted to outside engineering firms (see the diagram of the method used by CISTE-Rhône Poulenc, which is reproduced at the end of this section).

The main concern is to involve the future user at a very early stage in the project and to give him the role of client or specifier, from an overall administrative standpoint. The underlying strategy is to remember that it is the *user* who is most likely to be able to take a point of view that *combines* both the social and technical aspects.

☐ In Germany and the United Kingdom, more emphasis is placed on the *multidisciplinary* nature of design teams: the constitution of these teams must ensure that there is input from engineers, ergonomists, social scientists and labour experts ("Arbeitswissenschaftler").

☐ But the "project-management structure" does not simply consist of the design team or teams. From the outset, the *involvement of top management* is sought to define the guiding principles of the company philosophy which is to underlie the project.

This is what L E Davis refers to as the "policy committee", which may or may not coincide with the "steering committee" which is responsible for bringing together and involving all the managers whose areas of responsibility are affected by the project. These are also the bodies who select, direct, protect and support the design team.

A contractual relationship and a mandate reflecting confidence are of fundamental importance to an innovative, socio-technical approach. The quality and effectiveness of the design team's work depend to a large extent on the trust the team is afforded and on respect of its mandate by top management and the steering committee.

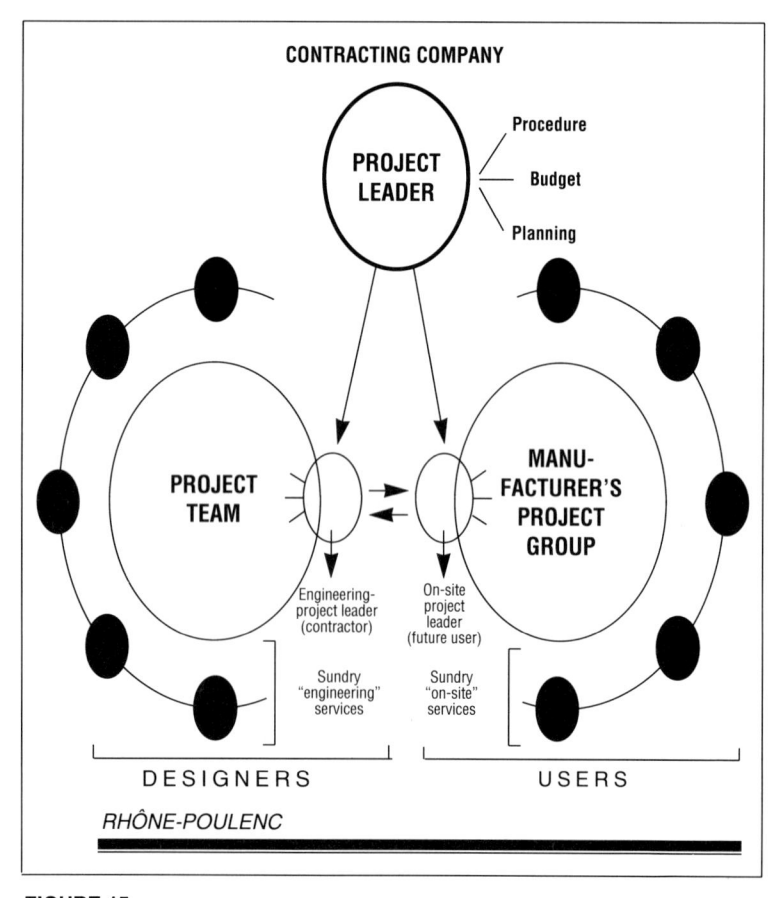

**FIGURE 15**

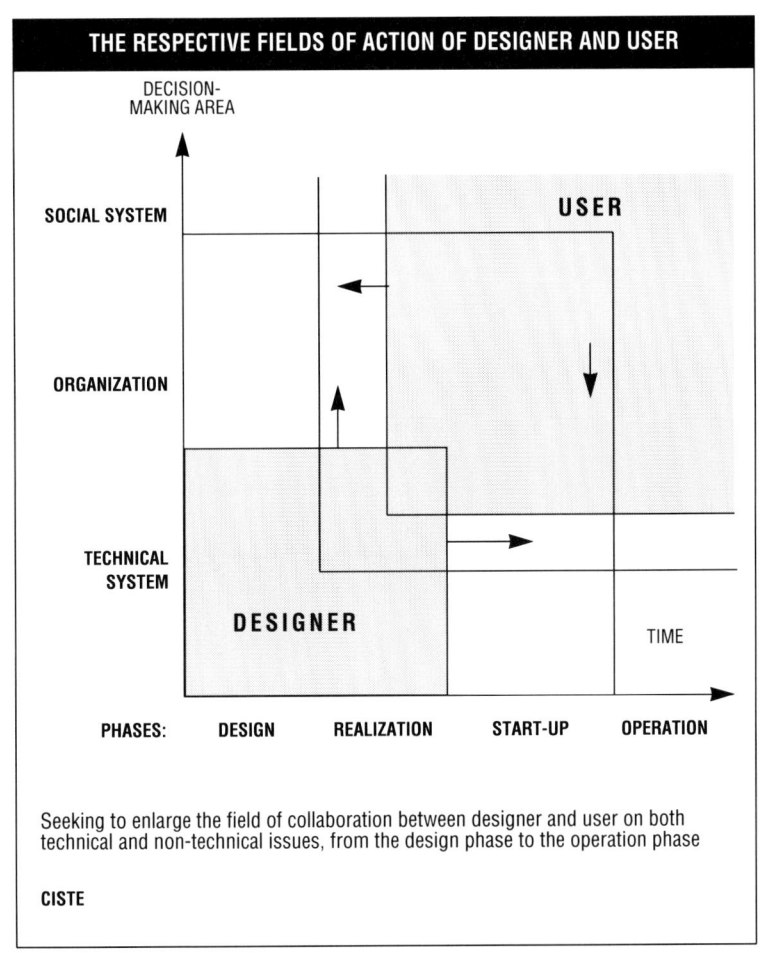

```
┌─────────────────────────────────────────────────────┐
│   THE RESPECTIVE FIELDS OF ACTION OF DESIGNER AND USER │
│                                                     │
│        DECISION-                                    │
│        MAKING AREA                                  │
│                                                     │
│   SOCIAL SYSTEM              USER                   │
│                                                     │
│   ORGANIZATION                                      │
│                                                     │
│   TECHNICAL                                         │
│   SYSTEM                                            │
│              DESIGNER              TIME             │
│                                                     │
│   PHASES:  DESIGN  REALIZATION  START-UP  OPERATION │
│                                                     │
│   Seeking to enlarge the field of collaboration between designer and user on both │
│   technical and non-technical issues, from the design phase to the operation phase │
│                                                     │
│   CISTE                                             │
└─────────────────────────────────────────────────────┘
```

**FIGURE 16**

The analysis grid reproduced on the next page (taken from O du Roy *et al*, "Réussir l'investissement" [Successful investment], p 108) is a suggested way in which the enterprise can define the desired level of participation by indicating for each of its departments one of four levels of involvement: inform, consult, involve in a participatory way, or involve as a body represented in the project team.

# THE FACTORY OF THE FUTURE

| Department or function | To be informed | To be consulted | To participate | To be represented in the project team | Occupation grades to be involved (workers, foremen, managers) | At which point in the project |
|---|---|---|---|---|---|---|
| Production | | | | | | |
| Quality assurance | | | | | | |
| Maintenance | | | | | | |
| Supplies | | | | | | |
| Methods | | | | | | |
| Administration | | | | | | |
| Data processing | | | | | | |
| Management | | | | | | |
| Personnel management | | | | | | |
| Training | | | | | | |
| Sales | | | | | | |
| Planning | | | | | | |
| Logistics | | | | | | |
| Energy | | | | | | |

Level of involvement

**FIGURE 17**

# The Factory of the Future
### Socio-technical Investment Management — European Methods

## Part Five

## User Participation

Participation in the design process must be distinguished from the negotiation/concertation sought by workers' representative bodies and trade unions. American authors tend to use a single term to cover these two concepts[1] but it is our opinion that, as far as most European countries are concerned, it is better to avoid confusing them.

Participation essentially concerns "future users", and in every approach we can see the desire to establish *a new method of involving users* in investment projects as a pivotal issue.

## The definition of "users"

Users are *on the one hand former users* with practical experience and an informal knowledge of the production process. They are the people who operated the old plants, which have some similarities with the new ones. Above all, they know what happens when the unexpected occurs, when unforeseen events arise and are inappropriately handled; theirs is a knowledge based on experience, a knowledge which is all too often ignored.

But *on the other hand* we are also talking about *future users*, the people who will be responsible for operating the new plant and who, whatever their former experience, can see the investment from the point of view of the practical user.

Finally, users represent *a range of occupational categories and viewpoints* which must be brought together and used in the search for new collaboration and co-operation, even though they often represent opposing and contradictory forces in the day-to-day production process.

□ Users are members of *different occupational categories*:

- factory managers, engineers and white-collar workers;
- foremen or team leaders;
- technicians and skilled workers;
- unskilled workers.

□ Users belong to various *different departments:*

- maintenance and toolshop;
- production;
- logistics and scheduling;
- quality control and laboratory;
- management;
- personnel management, etc.

In this respect or at this level, each user has a particular outlook, a particular occupational culture, a particular viewpoint which, rooted as it often is in old and recurring conflicts, makes him see the investment as a threat or as an opportunity.

## Reasons for user participation

It is generally agreed that there are four main reasons for involving users in a project at the earliest possible stage:

□ *to capitalize on their knowledge*, which is of vital importance to successful investment;

□ *to facilitate their training and preparation* for operating these new plants;

□ *to enable them to take over* new equipment, new workshop facilities, etc, by making them active participants in the change. This helps to limit the risk of their opposition to new plants;

☐ by making all these occupational categories and departments work together in creating their future world of work, *to devise, on an experimental basis, other methods of functioning and to establish cohesive teams.*

## The dynamics of participation

User participation in a project can be achieved only by taking a methodical approach and by questioning certain practices or procedures of investment management.

### The contracting enterprise's project team
The first step here is for the contracting enterprise or its on-site representative to set up a project team and appoint a project leader; the organizational structure of this team is usually the same as that of the contractor's team (representing the engineering firm or suppliers). This subject has already been covered in the chapter on the design team (Part Four).

### The participation of users at every level
The setting-up of the contracting enterprise's project team (or manufacturer's project group) is not the sole means of involving users in a project. It is merely a core structure around which participation on a broader scale can be co-ordinated.

The participation of blue- and white-collar employees, whatever their grade or occupation, and of the various different departments cannot be organized according to strict, unvarying rules. Participation and the way in which it is organized will vary depending on human relations and customary practices in each enterprise. It is not something that can simply be improvised when an investment is being made.

## INVOLVING USERS

### WHO?
- different levels (managers – specialists – workers)
- different departments (eg production, maintenance)

### WHY?
- to make use of their knowledge
- to facilitate their training
- to allow for adaptation
- to prepare new organizational structures

### HOW?
- project team consisting of users
- studies of real work
- participation
- operational specifications

**FIGURE 18**

**Working groups and simulation**
Participation can make three major contributions:

- in amassing expertise and gathering information on problems associated with the existing situation;

- in studying the technical project to select the appropriate options;

- in anticipating future conditions of operation.

These three functions are interlinked (see diagram). Working groups, led by the project team and sometimes assisted by outside experts, are very effective in this respect.

Technical problems need to be explained in a simple comprehensible way, particularly when the project involves new equipment or technology which is still uncommon. Aids such as models and clear diagrams of equipment, simple flow charts, axonometric views of workshops, and particularly visits to factories or suppliers, are essential supports for discussion.

If the future user is to make a valid contribution to "anticipating probable future work", he must be put in a situation in which he can envisage as clearly as possible what he will be doing, in a situation in which he can *envisage his own role*.

---

REFERENCES

1. See L E Davis, "Joint design of organizations and advanced technology in manufacturing", paper given in Venice at an RSO conference on "Joint design of technology, organization and people growth", p 11: "The creation of *participative* joint design methodology. Here employee representatives, union officials, technical and social science experts, and operational managers are all members of the joint Design Team".

# THE FACTORY OF THE FUTURE
SOCIO-TECHNICAL INVESTMENT MANAGEMENT
— EUROPEAN METHODS

## PART SIX

# THE ROLE OF WORKERS' REPRESENTATIVES AND TRADE-UNION ORGANIZATIONS

*Social negotiation* with workers' representatives should not be confused with *user participation*, which is why it is covered in a separate chapter here.

With regard to France, F Daniéllou writes:

> "It is essential to draw a clear distinction between the role of workers' statutory representatives and the direct contribution made by workers themselves.
>
> The role of statutory representative bodies (works councils and committees for health, safety and working conditions) is recognized and laid down by law. Members of these bodies are responsible for ensuring that the interests of the entire work-force are respected, both in the short and in the long term. Their legally recognized prerogatives when working methods are being changed bear both on working conditions and on the organization of work.
>
> The direct intervention of workers in a design process is of a different order. Each worker represents only his own view, but his specific occupational knowledge and skills are of vital importance. When production or maintenance workers, electricians, foremen, etc, are invited to join forces to assess the design and operation of a machine, their different viewpoints combine to form an overall picture, which means the group can make a valuable contribution to the design.
>
> Informing/consulting workers' representatives and directly involving workers in the design process are not, therefore, mutually exclusive. On the contrary, they should be carefully combined and co-ordinated. If provision is made for the setting-up of working groups

whose members include workers, then workers' representative bodies should be informed and consulted as regards the objectives and functioning of these groups."[1]

Socio-technical methods of project management draw the partners involved in social negotiation into new forms of negotiation so that, instead of discussing the *social impact* of technical investments after the event, they discuss a socio-technical project right from the start.

If we need to distinguish between the role of workers' representative bodies and user participation, we need also to identify a *third role* — that of trade-union organizations.

The social context varies from one country to another, and there are strategic differences between the various trade-union organizations within each country.

Without wishing to speak for them, it could be said that trade-union organizations tend to take up certain positions with respect to their role in participatory management processes.

## Co-ordinating action at national and local level

It is standard practice for trade-union organizations representing workers *in a particular industry* to take steps to co-ordinate progress towards an effective participation process, both through agreements covering individual establishments and through industry agreements (or company agreements or agreements covering several establishments), so that worker participation becomes the general norm rather than merely being the prerogative of workers in very large enterprises. "Framework agreements" may be negotiated to encourage the development of the participation process (eg the framework agreement covering the French chemicals industry).

## Ensuring that all workers benefit from the participation process and from social progress

The processes of enriched project management usually concern only a small proportion of workers at a given industrial establishment, though it is not uncommon for the modernization of a particular workshop to be accompanied by restructuring (and, therefore, problems concerning jobs and retraining) in other workshops in the same establishment.

In many countries, the remit of trade-union organizations is to protect the interests of *all* workers at a given establishment. This means they cannot allow the workers they represent to be subjected to a "two-speed democracy" depending on the workshop in which they are employed. They therefore tend, quite naturally, to raise issues concerning the status, future and involvement of all the other workers in the establishment when they are discussing the question of the participation of workers affected by a particular project.

In the eyes of trade-union organizations, these two dimensions need to be considered together, and *enriched* project management must imply *enriched* industrial relations in general. The belief that an enterprise should be modernized *using the available work-force* at the establishment is in any case becoming increasingly popular among both technical experts and employers alike.

This calls for retraining, the adaptation of skills, forward management of the age structure of the work-force, etc, throughout the enterprise. These are all issues that trade-union organizations want to discuss with the employer in advance.

## Negotiating the details of implementation of the project

This approach, regarding which we have very little practical experience or methodological literature, except in the case of countries in which industrial relations are based on the concept of "joint management", involves:

☐ early negotiation;

☐ advance negotiation of the participation process: objectives and methods;

☐ advance negotiation of choices with regard to work organization.

### Early negotiation

The first step in ensuring that workers' representative bodies are able to play a role that complies with the spirit of a socio-technical approach is to involve them at an earlier stage than is the norm. This means *informing* them of a project when there is still margin for manoeuvre with respect to real *choices*, not simply as regards the *social implications* (staffing, skill levels, pay, working conditions, etc) but also as regards the technical aspects of the project. This is the only way in which workers' representatives can make a real contribution to optimizing both the social and the technical system, which means they must be informed of the project and its economic purpose.

The problem for the trade unions in this new negotiation scenario is that the greater their involvement during the early stages of a project and on a level other than a purely social one, the greater their implication in the economic aspect of that project, even if it is merely to point out opposing or additional interests and objectives. This approach to negotiation is similar to that of joint management.

### Advance negotiation of the participation process: objectives and methods

In socio-technical investment management, nothing is fixed from the start: each stage of the project explores different alternatives and a synthesized approach is gradually developed. Initial negotiations will, therefore, bear more on:

- ☐ the situation at the beginning of the project: problems and objectives;

- ☐ the blueprint that will allow gradual development of the project and consideration, at each of its stages, of the viewpoints of workers and their representatives.

### The situation at the beginning of the project: problems and objectives

Trade-union organizations are in a better position to identify the various issues involved in a project if they are well informed. In the enriched management approach, the criteria for deciding whether or not to go ahead with an investment depend on criteria of which they are in control.

For example, they may need to devote more attention to some "pilot projects" than others; some may proceed more smoothly even though they are more restricted in scope; some may directly concern employment, job security, the working environment or new job classifications.

### Advance negotiation of the participation blueprint

Trade-union organizations want to have the opportunity to express their views on the quality of the participation processes proposed by the employer. They may feel that some of the methods or structures to be used are inappropriate, or token gestures.

This means that trade-union organizations have a valid contribution to make to the planning of enriched *projects*:

☐ With regard to the actual *blueprint*: its organization and structure as regards participation.

What form of project organization would, at each stage of the project, allow:
— workers to express their opinions;
— workers' representative bodies to monitor the process, to be informed and involved;
— trade-union organizations to negotiate "in time"?

How should the project be scheduled?

What structures of participation should be used?

What roles should be assigned to the various actors, and in particular to trade-union organizations, in the negotiation process?

☐ With regard to the *methods* used with regard to working groups which include workers:

How should working groups be organized?
How should their scope be defined?
How are the proposals put forward by these groups to be studied?
Will designers receive their proposals in time?
How are any disagreements to be resolved?
How should working groups be constituted?

In this regard, trade-union organizations may feel that some methods are better than others and may want to involve their own experts to ensure that the best methods are used.

☐ With regard to *means*:

To what information and training are workers' delegates and trade-union representatives entitled?

What means are to be used for exchanging information and assessing similar projects at other establishments?

How and to what extent should experts be called upon to help workers' delegates and trade-union representatives to make a valid and timely contribution to the project?

What financial incentives will be available for the social partners involved in this process?

☐ With regard to the socio-technical *evaluation* of the innovations introduced:

Analysis of experiences of "enriched project management" has led trade-union organizations to call for the drafting of evaluation blueprints that allow the various social partners to assess any new project.

This could be the subject of an agreement. Agreements of this kind would certainly allow for the identification of social and technical *indicators* which could be monitored over time. Such project evaluations would be invaluable to the social partners because future policy could draw lessons from them without the social partners abandoning their *roles*.

## Advance negotiation of choices with regard to work organization

In the past, trade-union organizations have often intervened *after the event* to negotiate the *outcome* for workers of the technical and organizational choices made (job classification, pay, etc).

Some organizations now want to negotiate *sooner* (ie at an early stage of the project) and to be involved in making the technical choices which predetermine, or make it very difficult to reverse, choices affecting the organization of work or of the work-force with which they disagree and which they would, therefore, like to alter by negotiation.

Admittedly this raises problems regarding areas of competence and innovation for all the social partners, but nonetheless it seems to be the only possible way forward.

## Perceiving and making full use of the opportunities afforded by each stage of the project to broaden the field of negotiation

According to this approach, negotiation must be co-ordinated with the various stages of the project and be based on the opportunities afforded by each of those stages. It must also take account of the *uncertainties* inherent in an industrial project and must not demand certainties and guarantees before project studies have been completed. This is why it is so important to discuss the project process rather than *a priori* conclusions, which is in turn why it is important to time negotiations according to the state of progress of the project.

Figure 19 shows an example of such a structure of negotiation, proposed as a model by some Dutch authors writing of a socially inventive process of automation.[2]

Similar forms of negotiation are already widely practised in countries such as Sweden and the Federal Republic of Germany.[3] In France too, the branch of the union CFDT (Confédération Française Démocratique de Travail) covering the chemicals industry has published

THE FACTORY OF THE FUTURE

**Formal negotiation integrated in a project**

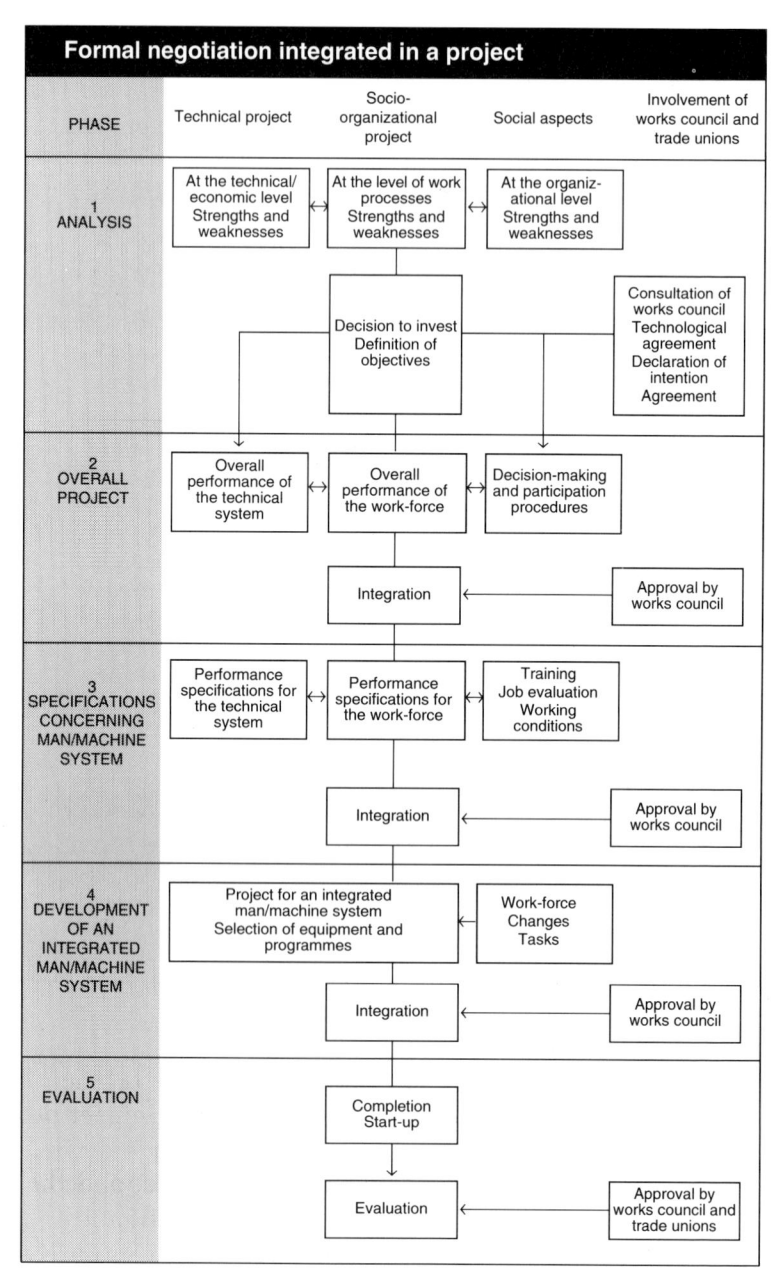

| PHASE | Technical project | Socio-organizational project | Social aspects | Involvement of works council and trade unions |
|---|---|---|---|---|
| 1 ANALYSIS | At the technical/economic level Strengths and weaknesses | At the level of work processes Strengths and weaknesses | At the organizational level Strengths and weaknesses | |
| | | Decision to invest Definition of objectives | | Consultation of works council Technological agreement Declaration of intention Agreement |
| 2 OVERALL PROJECT | Overall performance of the technical system | Overall performance of the work-force | Decision-making and participation procedures | |
| | | Integration | | Approval by works council |
| 3 SPECIFICATIONS CONCERNING MAN/MACHINE SYSTEM | Performance specifications for the technical system | Performance specifications for the work-force | Training Job evaluation Working conditions | |
| | | Integration | | Approval by works council |
| 4 DEVELOPMENT OF AN INTEGRATED MAN/MACHINE SYSTEM | | Project for an integrated man/machine system Selection of equipment and programmes | Work-force Changes Tasks | |
| | | Integration | | Approval by works council |
| 5 EVALUATION | | Completion Start-up | | |
| | | Evaluation | | Approval by works council and trade unions |

**FIGURE 19**

guidelines for negotiation within the framework of technical investment projects.[4]

These methods still meet resistance both from employers and from trade unions. Yet they encourage the social partners to work together in tackling issues that could lead to the emergence of new social practices. Some possible ways forward have already been identified by the Riboud report and in the discussions it generated.[5] ANACT has also set out some guidelines for this new approach to social negotiation integrated with technological change:

> "Negotiation of new technologies must, as far as possible, be co-ordinated with the process of technical design, and should continue throughout the design process and until the new plant is operating 'normally'."

This has several consequences:

- firstly, the actual form of negotiation changes (...), since (...) exchange procedures are developed in which various points of view are put forward and alternatives examined. Express agreement can then be reached regarding the *objectives* of such a concerted approach, (...) the *method* of dealing with problems (...) and, of course, the *impact* of the project on certain aspects of the situation of workers (...);

- negotiation assumes that it is possible, on the basis of the project, to *anticipate* the impact of a given choice or decision on work and workers. This is never entirely possible, and the earlier negotiations begin the more difficult such anticipation becomes. Yet if there is no anticipation of margins for manoeuvre, there is

63

no real negotiation: "persuasion is not the same as negotiation".[6]

---

REFERENCES

1. "Les modalités d'une ergonomie de conception" (Methods of ergonomic design), INRS, Notes Documentaires, No. 129, winter 1987
2. A A F Brouwers, F Vaas and F D Pot, "Sociaal Inventief Automatiseren, Integratie van Arbeid en Techniek in de Ontwerpfase" (Socially inventive automation, integration of work and technology in the design phase), FNV Steunpunt Technologie, Amsterdam, 1987, pp 44-47
3. See, for example, the guidelines for works councils drafted by IG Metall: "Beteiligung des Betriebsrats bei betrieblichen Humanisierungsvorhaben" (Works-council participation in company humanization plans), 1980
4. "Négocier les changements du travail" (Negotiating changes in work), Editions INPACT, Paris, 1989
5. Antoine Riboud, "Modernisation mode d'emploi, rapport au Premier Ministre" (The modernization of working methods: report to the Prime Minister), Paris, Union Générale d'Editions, No. 10/18, 1987: Chapter 2 — Repenser l'investissement productif (Rethinking investment in production), which is largely based on "Réussir l'investissement productif"; and Chapter 4.1 — L'impératif de la négociation (The imperative of negotiation), pp 109-113. See also "Moderniser les entreprises" (Modernizing enterprises), INT conference volume, Lyons, 28/29 June 1988; and in particular the paper by Y Lichtenberger, "La négociation des changements technologiques dans l'entreprise" (The negotiation of technological changes in an enterprise), pp 37-41
6. P-L Rémy, "Changements technologiques et négociations" (Technological change and negotiation), in ANACT's newsletter, No. 133, September 1988, p 5

# THE FACTORY OF THE FUTURE
## SOCIO-TECHNICAL INVESTMENT MANAGEMENT — EUROPEAN METHODS

## PART SEVEN

# STUDIES OF EXISTING SITUATIONS AS "REFERENCE SITUATIONS"

The use of "studies of existing situations" or of the current state of affairs is a constant in the socio-technical approach to investment. We shall not give details of the methods used, which do not essentially differ from those applied in any *improvement scheme*. Four points should, however, be emphasized:

- *ergonomics*, the practical rather than theoretical science of work;
- the role of *reference situations*;
- the importance of *variables or contingent factors*;
- the *informal* knowledge of users.

## Use of "reference situations"

The notion of "reference situations" comes straight from the ergonomic teachings of A Wisner, who said at the October 1976 conference of SELF (Société d'Ergonomie de Langue Française): "The ergonomics of organization (...) teaches all those concerned to practise good ergonomics of design". The conducting, in accordance with the teachings of the CNAM school of ergonomics, of an analysis of real work in a workshop situation has induced this caution with regard to a purely theoretical approach to ergonomics.

In 1979, we wrote in "L'ingénierie et les conditions de travail" (Engineering and working conditions)[1] of the importance "of making design teams aware of the constraints recognized as a result of work experience in *reference factories*".

Similarly, concluding the analysis of a design case study, we wrote:

> "It is only real work situations that can serve as a basis for ergonomic and socio-technical

recommendations within the framework of a project (as *reference situations*), which can be used to make the necessary extrapolations and transpositions.

"Such situations usually exist, or situations can be found that have similarities with those planned."[2]

Since then, the notion has become a constant feature of all the similar methods discussed.[3] What we need to do is both to take account of "real work", with all its variable and contingent factors, as it is experienced by the operator on the shopfloor and not as idealized or modelled by the design engineer, and to consider technical innovations to improve the situation. Hence the methods of *anticipation* and *simulation* proposed by the authors of socio-technical handbooks.[4]

## Ergonomics: the study of real work

One of the areas of knowledge that has the most to contribute to socio-technical management of investment projects is ergonomics. It is, said A Wisner, a technology rather than a science, meaning by this to place it on the same level as the engineering knowledge with which it must be combined.

The contribution made by ergonomics may take various forms:

☐ Ergonomics is, first and foremost, knowledge and analysis of *real work* in "reference situations". As a result of these analyses, *specifications* can be enriched to take account of the constraints associated with the workforce's real activities.

☐ It is also the analysis of plant plans and technical projects from the point of view of *foreseeable operational difficulties:* accessibility for maintenance, room for movement around plants, risks and hazards, the visibility of operations, and anticipation of work constraints under poor conditions (breakdown, change-overs, start-up, manual operations, etc).

☐ Finally, ergonomics implies consideration of *normative constraints* on design, particularly as regards man-machine interfaces: commands, signals, etc.

The ANACT publication "Conduite de projet" (Project management), in summarizing Daniéllou's recommendations,[5] lays down some excellent guidelines for the ergonomic design of operating systems:[6]

- layout of information and controls;
- ergonomics of equipment (desks, keyboards, screens);
- ergonomics of the software of man/system interfaces;
- design of alarms and warnings.

But it is evidently not enough to impose theoretical standards which "do not allow for consideration of the specific characteristics of tasks in the future workshop".[7] Which sends us back to the analysis of reference situations and the simulation of probable future activity.

## The user's informal knowledge: knowledge of variable and contingent factors

In addition to the experts' knowledge and application of ergonomics, socio-technical methods of project management all in their own way recommend the involvement in the project of *users*, meaning future users: engineers, foremen and workers. Every effort is

# STUDIES OF EXISTING SITUATIONS AS "REFERENCE SITUATIONS"

**CISTE**

**DESIGN OF PLANTS**
**ENVISAGED WORK**

**DESIGNERS' VIEWPOINT**

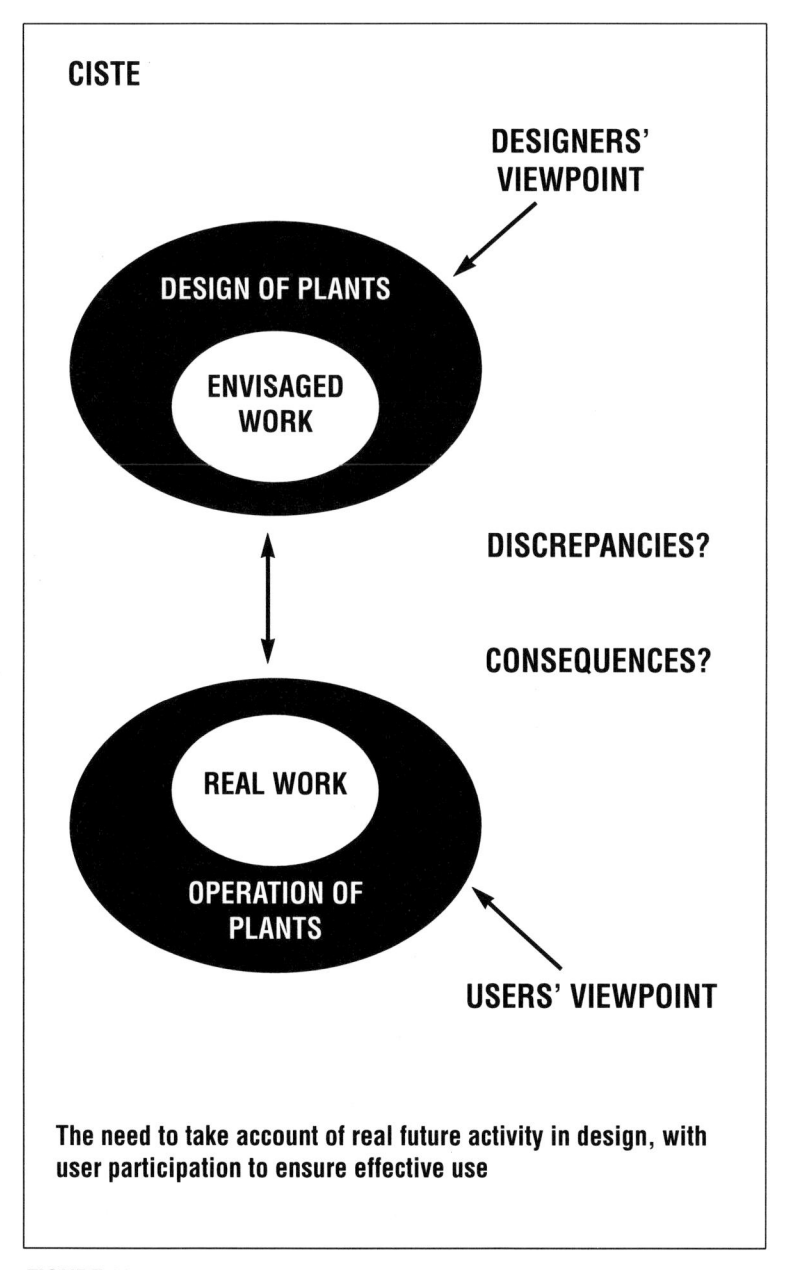

**DISCREPANCIES?**

**CONSEQUENCES?**

**REAL WORK**
**OPERATION OF PLANTS**

**USERS' VIEWPOINT**

The need to take account of real future activity in design, with user participation to ensure effective use

**FIGURE 20**

made to ensure that these people, who are largely ignored by traditional, purely technical methods, have a say at as early a stage as possible.

This may give rise to two questions:

☐ how to make them participate in the various stages and what form that participation is going to take;

☐ how to facilitate dialogue between users and designers.

- The first step in *making users participate* is to question them on their experience of production, maintenance and management in the reference situations of which they have direct or indirect knowledge. This involves gathering, formalizing and assessing the user's "informal knowledge", which is knowledge of risks, contingencies and variables, as well as of responses to them, which are often instinctive or "based on experience".

  The next step is to apply this experience to the future situation, ie when the project has been completed, using either a diagram or, in preference, a model. This can lead to anticipation of problems (see above, p 37).

- *Facilitating dialogue* between users and designers involves helping users not to express themselves in terms of a solution, but rather to translate their language of experience or of the solution (which is like a narrative account) into the language of the performance objective (which is the language of the technical specifications). This requires extensive support and often the mediation of an expert.[8]

Socio-technical methods of analysing production operations have always made use of studies of variable and contingent factors. It is in fact the way in which contingencies are handled that is the real test of the quality of a socio-technical system. Unforeseen events also reveal problems (critical-incidents method). This is what makes socio-technical organization so much better than any other type of organization — it integrates the ability of the human operator to cope with the unexpected. But this means that work situations on the one hand, and organizations and the knowledge (or theoretical frames of reference) of operators on the other, must have been designed to facilitate such adjustments and to make it possible to take the right decisions at the right time.

REFERENCES

1  Article published in "La revue de l'entreprise", 1979, p 50
2  In "Intégration des méthodes ergonomiques et socio-techniques dans la conception d'une usine nouvelle" (Integration of ergonomic and socio-technical methods in the design of a new factory), DGRST report, 1980. From the same period, F Jankovsky and M Piazza, "Méthodologie de l'ergonomie dans la conception industrielle" (Methodology of ergonomics in industrial design), DGRST. SERI, pp 112 and 123: "ergonomics must find a comparable situation to serve as a reference situation".
3  "Réussir l'investissement" (Successful investment), pp 71-75; "Conduite de projet" (Project management), pp 32-35
4  "Réussir l'investissement", p 32: Simulating future operation; "L'opérateur, la vanne, l'écran" (The operator, the valve and the screen), pp 187-195; "Conduite de projet", pp 29-33: Probable future activity, and p 92: "What if" meetings
5  In "L'opérateur, la vanne et l'écran", pp 263-341
6  In "Conduite de projet", pp 117-124
7  "Conduite de projet", p 123
8  C Midler has noted that every method uses mediation between the technical specialist and the user (in an article in "Gérer et Comprendre, Annales des Mines", March 1989, No. 14, entitled "De l'automatisation à la modernisation: les transformations dans l'industrie automobile, 2° Episode: vers de nouvelles pratiques de gestion des projets industriels" [From automation to modernization: changes in the automotive industry; Part 2: towards new methods of managing industrial projects])

# THE FACTORY OF THE FUTURE
SOCIO-TECHNICAL INVESTMENT MANAGEMENT
— EUROPEAN METHODS

# PART EIGHT

# SOCIO-TECHNICAL SPECIFICATIONS

The BSN method[1] placed particular emphasis on the development of *socio-organizational objectives* expressed with the force of technical specifications and having equal weight and importance, in terms of "performance standards and objectives", to the exclusion of the ways and means of achieving those objectives.

- This *mastery of the "language of technical designers"* by users as well as specialists in the social sciences and labour experts has come to be seen as essential if there is to be dialogue between users and designers, whose relationship is deemed to be one of client/supplier.

  Production staff do in fact tend to talk in terms of *technical solutions* rather than in terms of "technical or social specifications", ie in terms of performance objectives or the *output* of a system. This amounts to defining the "mould" of the system required, defining it by the desired or intended results, which leaves designers maximum margin for manoeuvre in their work.

- *This means placing social requirements (organization, skill levels, working conditions) on the same level as technical requirements* and expressing them in the same language (the language of specifications). Expressing requirements in terms of objectives is a distinct advantage at several significant points in an investment project:

  ☐ when the basic objectives of the project are being defined;

  ☐ when invitations to tender are being sent to suppliers of studies and technologies.

## When the basic objectives of the project are being defined

The project charter or the mandate given to the project team by the enterprise's management should define both the technical and economic objectives and the socio-organizational objectives of the project. This is the best way of ensuring that studies take account of the constraints implied by the two-fold nature of the project's objectives, and of making decisions based on both types of criteria.

## Example of a factory project based on socio-organizational objectives

"The organization of the factory must take account of the following objectives:

- ☐ to use *a work-force with higher skill levels*;

- ☐ *to reduce the number of occupational grades*: just one intermediate level between workers and department heads;

- ☐ work and organizational methods will stress the importance of *workers expressing their opinions and taking part in decision-making processes*, which will be facilitated by the setting-up of working groups and regular meetings;

- ☐ *to decentralize, at the level of operational departments, functions* associated with quality, supplies, production management, personnel management, maintenance, training and information technology;

- ☐ to integrate *training* as an ongoing process."

To these organizational objectives, which were set out at the same time as the technical-performance programme, were added:

- ☐ ergonomic constraints;

☐ constraints concerning the environment and architecture.

Another example of organizational objectives being laid down at the outset of an investment project is that of a project involving Courage's Berkshire Brewery, which was followed by Albert Cherns.

We shall see that the objectives here (which are more closely linked to fundamental options or the philosophy of the organization) bear on the approach as well as the "end-product".

"The key elements of this philosophy are:

- in planning and implementing the project, to make use of existing channels of *communication and consultation* so as to involve as many people as possible in the project;

- to make use of the considerable experience and expertise available at all levels within the company to launch the new brewery, and to provide all the necessary background information;

- to draw up contracts and terms and conditions of employment that will make people feel personally involved in the brewery's success and in increased sales of its products;

- to ensure that all jobs are adapted to suit individuals, are accessible and offer the greatest possible opportunity for career development within the company;

- to provide a healthy, efficient and pleasant working environment, making use of the best possible advice and practical experience available;

- to encourage good relations with the local community and run the factory so that it provides benefits for both the town and the company."

German methods[2] reflect a wish to base projects on multiple objectives. Here, for example, is a systematic presentation of the different areas to be taken into account:

| COSTS | ORGANIZATION | WORK-FORCE | DEADLINES |
|---|---|---|---|
| Material costs | Length of production cycle | Working conditions | Beginning of studies |
| Wage costs | Physical flow | Retraining | End of studies |
| General costs | Flexibility | Motivation | Interim evaluation |
| Quality costs | Information flow | Turn-over, absenteeism | Beginning of operation |
| Maintenance costs | Use of equipment | Non-productive time | End of operation |
| Management costs | Stocks | Payment system | Final evaluation |
| New technology | Plant | Personnel management | |

**MAIN DESIGN OBJECTIVES**

These objectives are also reflected in the criteria laid down to allow for the devising of alternatives (see p 82).

*When invitations to tender are being sent out to suppliers*, it is very advantageous to oblige them to make commitments regarding performance and price *including* consideration of social and ergonomic objectives.

## Example: in a project concerning a new food factory

The order for new packing plants was preceded by a study of existing lines of the same technical generation already being used in the group. The tender specifications based on these studies included operational as well as technical constraints.

Here are some examples of the "socio-technical specifications" included:

"The operator must have visual information on the quality of the seal and, where action is required, the block must be easily removable to allow easy cleaning of the sealing heads...

The operator must have information on temperature and pressure levels and must be able to regulate them.

The constructor will identify the main control point from which the foreman can:

- ☐ monitor production, in either a sitting or standing position, without having to move;
- ☐ take action without moving from the control area..."

---

REFERENCES

1 See "Réussir l'investissement productif", p 137 *et seq*
2 Example of the method: Arbeitsstrukturierung/Planungssystematik (structuring of work/planning system) (AEG-Telefunken, 1980)

SOCIO-TECHNICAL SPECIFICATIONS

**Examples of specifications clauses concerning organization and working conditions**

**TABLE 22**

...the block must be easily removable to allow easy cleaning of the sealing heads.

# THE FACTORY OF THE FUTURE

The operator must be able to load packs without raising her arms above her shoulders.

# The Factory of the Future
## Socio-technical Investment Management — European Methods

# Part Nine

## Identifying Alternatives

The creation of technical and organizational alternatives and combinations thereof (joint design or joint optimization) is one of the fundamental requirements of socio-technical methods.

There are several reasons for this:

- It is essential to create some "play" in the *margin for manoeuvre* to temper and rationalize the impact of technical aspects and to loosen the stranglehold of technical constraints on the social system. This is why it is necessary to prove that there is more than one way of achieving the desired objective.

- Working in accordance with *objectives* and under the constraint of multiple objectives usually opens the field. It is also of value as a test to see whether work is being conducted on the basis of objectives or on that of pure linear deduction.

- The notion of multiple alternatives is a highly recommendable *creative* approach if innovation is being sought in the joint design of the organization and of technology.

- Creating alternatives makes it possible to present and discuss a range of solutions with the final decision-maker, giving him real *freedom of choice in his decision* by making him look at his objectives and criteria without involving him in devising actual solutions. A decision based on alternatives is, therefore, more meaningful and attractive to management.

- Playing with alternatives also prevents the design team from focusing on a single solution, developing it to the full and defending it at any price. By spending too much time and energy on this single solution, there is a risk that the decision-making process will be distorted and, finally, if its preferred solution is rejected, that the design team will lose all motivation.

*German methods* of designing "work systems" place particular emphasis on the development of alternatives. Their success here rests on the fact that their first concern is to define highly operational design objectives, which they refer to as *criteria*. Once these criteria have been defined and considered, "initial solutions" are sought.

"The design and construction of an optimal work system require the identification and consideration of all possible solutions. *At least three* different work structures must be devised as initial solutions."[1]

The general layout of these methods clearly shows the phase at the beginning of a project in which objectives, criteria and alternatives are defined (see p 84, Figure 21, stages 2 and 3).

This same wish to create alternatives is found in the VDI method, which concentrates more particularly on the choice of the level of automation.

## A critical issue: choosing the level and mode of automation

The level and mode of automation represent a particular problem for both organizational and technical designers constructing a socio-technical organization:

☐ Which tasks are to be entrusted to human operators and which to the system?

☐ How is the human operator to guide the system?

# THE FACTORY OF THE FUTURE

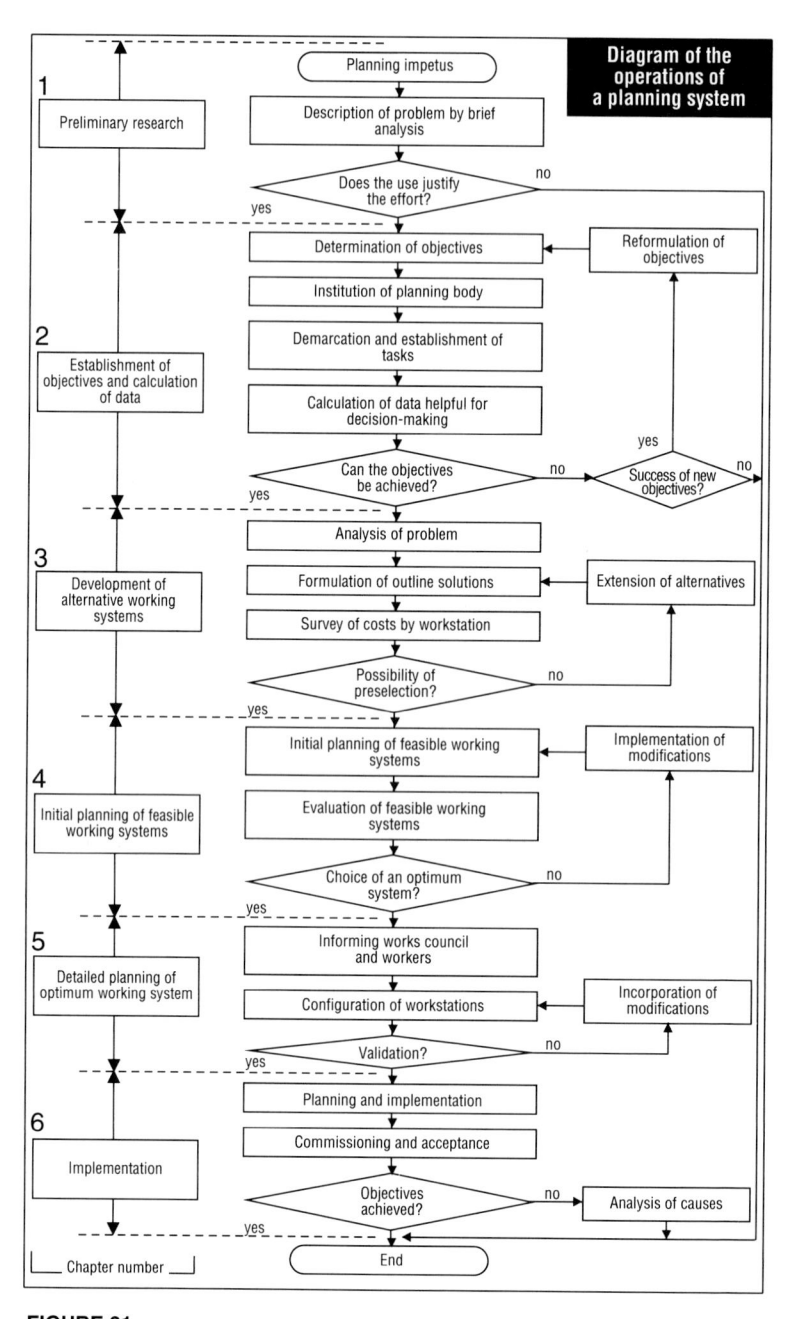

**FIGURE 21**

The problem derives from the division of labour between man and machine, and from the actual design of work. The Germans have developed a particularly good method of considering this issue by studying, in parallel, various solutions that optimize the use of technology and at the same time seek to make the best possible use of the human work-force. The flow chart below (Figure 22), which is taken from the VDI work already cited, illustrates this method of "dual design", which is in fact a dialectic form of joint design arising from the alternative to "full automation" (Sozialverträgliche Gestaltung von Automatisierungsvorhaben, pp 8-9).

"The method of 'dual design' is suggested for this parallel process of defining work and technology. Dual design is a principle based on:

☐ the optimization of technology;

☐ the optimum use of labour.

Organizational possibilities and the content of human work are consequently discussed in parallel with technology.

**DUAL DESIGN OF MAN-MACHINE SYSTEMS**

Production of ideas and of a project focusing on technology

Ideas

Ideas

Full automation
Partial automation
Computerization

"Manual"

KDI

Production of ideas and of a project focusing on human activity

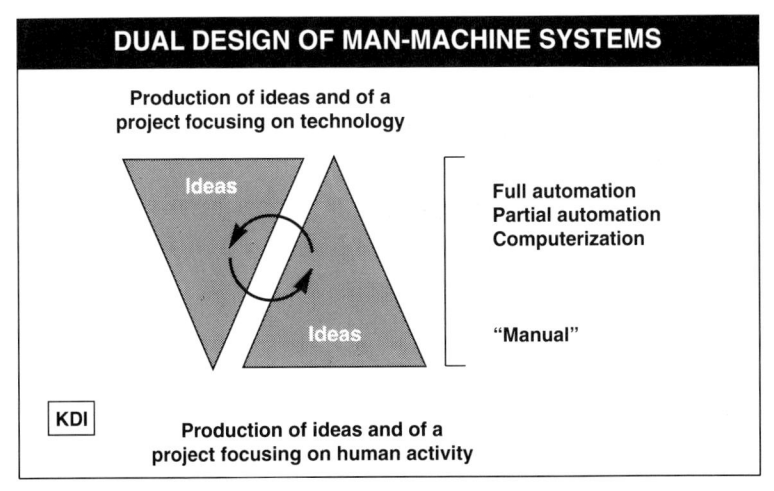

FIGURE 22     THE DUAL-DESIGN PRINCIPLE

All the basic activities of the automation project must first be specified. It is advisable to use a staged process for the structuring, performance and co-ordination of the various basic activities.

Two application projects need to be developed in parallel at each stage of development:

- a project focusing on human activity, in which every attempt is made to design work which is as skilled and motivating as possible, by optimizing the organization and structuring of work;
- a project focusing on technology, in which various possible automation designs are compared.

One of the essential factors of dual design is designers' willingness and ability to develop a whole range of different ideas concerning technical and manual possibilities — ideas that may be little more than "visions" at the beginning of the design process. They then evolve into proposals for appropriate solutions.

The two types of solution must be linked in a repetitive process. This is done by establishing a permanent exchange of the two modes of consideration and by a constant linking and comparison of the two perspectives."

Volkswagen documents and practices describe an application of this method. See Figure 23, next page.

# IDENTIFYING ALTERNATIVES

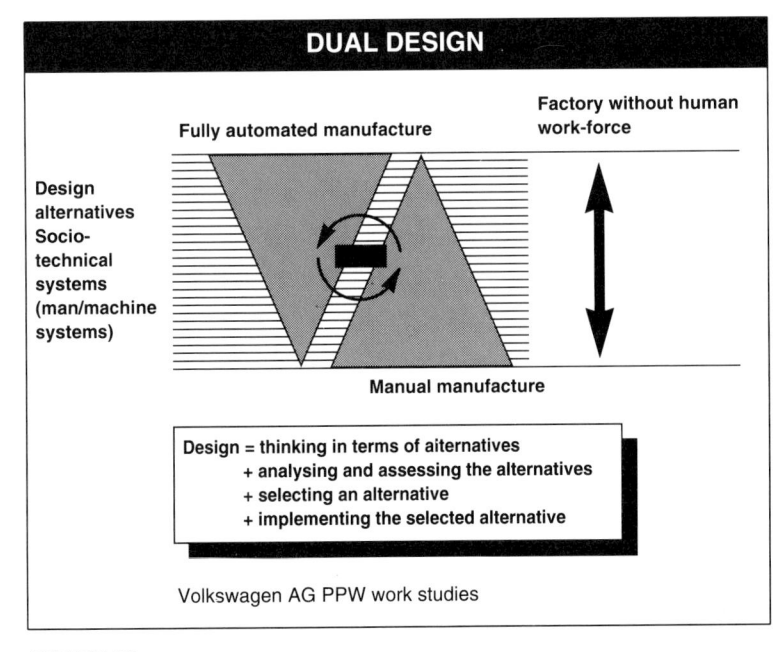

**FIGURE 23**

Dual Design

- Fully automated manufacture
- Factory without human work-force
- Manual manufacture

Design alternatives Socio-technical systems (man/machine systems)

Design = thinking in terms of alternatives
+ analysing and assessing the alternatives
+ selecting an alternative
+ implementing the selected alternative

Volkswagen AG PPW work studies

---

REFERENCES

1  AEG-Telefunken methods, as already cited p 77

# The Factory of the Future
## Socio-technical Investment Management — European Methods

# Part Ten

# The Organization at the Design Stage

The construction of an organization cannot be reduced, as is often the case in industrial projects, to estimating the work-force's productivity and drawing up an organization chart. It is a far richer and more complicated process.

Other areas of knowledge are brought to bear to enrich the sciences and technologies of the engineer: the knowledge of the organization specialist or socio-technical expert, ie specialists in the functioning of organizations.

It is important to recognize this area of knowledge, too long confused with that of the methodologist, who is merely a technician specializing in human labour that can be mechanized. Nor is it the same as the knowledge of the sociologist of industrial organizations, who merely analyses existing structures and the changes affecting them.

This knowledge leads not only to the identification of alternatives in relation to available systems, but also to an understanding of the possible effects of these choices on job satisfaction, potential conflicts and the areas of responsibility of the various people involved.

## Philosophy of the organization: basic options

The construction of an organization implies the selection, at the outset, of a number of objectives or, better still, values — what the Americans call the *philosophy of the organization*.

Central to the construction of an organization is the choice of *a principle of responsibility* or "responsibilization":

What does one do to ensure that individuals or groups achieve their objectives, adapt to contingencies and variables in their environment, improve their work, make progress or ensure the continuity of work?

Does one set up a system of hierarchical or operational *rules and regulations*? Does one depend on contractual agreements? Or does one look to responsible autonomy?

## The nature of the organization constructed is dependent on the approach adopted in the project

It is important to construct the organization according to *a process which is consistent with the final structure sought*: if the desired end result is a responsible, flexible organization which is capable of adapting of its own accord to changes in its environment and which is open to the personal participation and investment of all concerned, it is best to construct it with the participation of those people from the outset. The construction process or approach taken are as important as the nature of the organization, because they determine it.

## Six key elements of an organization, which must be integrated at the design stage

The design of an organization, from the socio-technical viewpoint, consists of bringing together, at the design stage, human and material resources to form coherent systems in which people have a sense of involvement and responsibility.

L E Davis proposes the expansion of "self-maintaining organizational units" to create units capable of achieving their objectives in a varied and uncertain environment. What we need to do is to determine the appropriate size and boundaries of these units.

There seem to be six key elements in this "construction" of an organization which offers both flexibility and a sense of responsibility:

## The distribution of support functions

We need to decide how to distribute or group production-support functions such as maintenance, logistics, management and quality control. Organizations based on Taylorism divided these functions to form separate departments, thus contributing to the fragmentation of work and the emergence of major conflicts of objectives.

Ulbo de Sitter's diagram[1] clearly illustrates the distribution of support functions in new organizations.

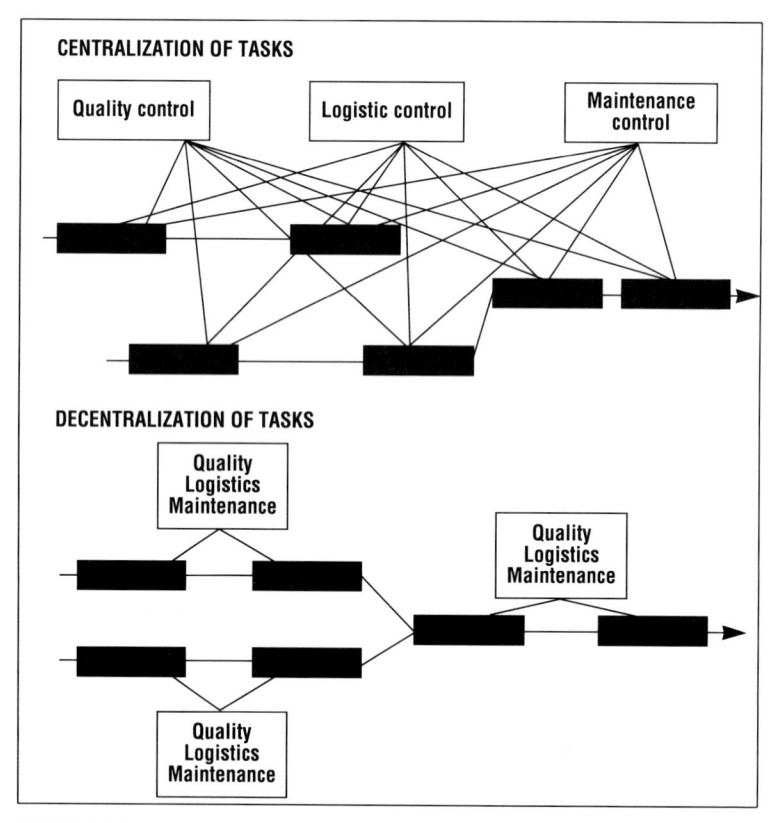

**FIGURE 24**      **GLOBALIZATION**

But this global approach to the organization is not enough; it is also important to reintegrate tasks of preparation, maintenance and management in employees' work.

**Size and grouping of units**
The question of tracing the boundaries between units in the production process itself is closely linked to the distribution of support functions. Human and material resources need to be grouped in such a way as to minimize interfaces and dependence, thus forming sub-units whose output is significant in itself and therefore gives members of the unit a sense of responsibility.

Different solutions may be reached, depending on the products and technologies involved:

- integrated production lines;

- workshops using particular technologies or performing particular processes.

De Sitter proposes a dual strategy to obtain a flexible organization: *parallelization* and *segmentation*, in addition to the *globalization* of functions described earlier (see Figure 24):[2]

In any event, consideration needs to be given to the optimum size of production units and teams in relation to several parameters which should be optimized:

- technology and tools;

- products or sub-units;

- type of skills to be brought together;

- the possibility of creating a sense of responsibility.

# THE FACTORY OF THE FUTURE

**CHOICE OF FLOW ORGANIZATION**

Transverse organization, by specialism

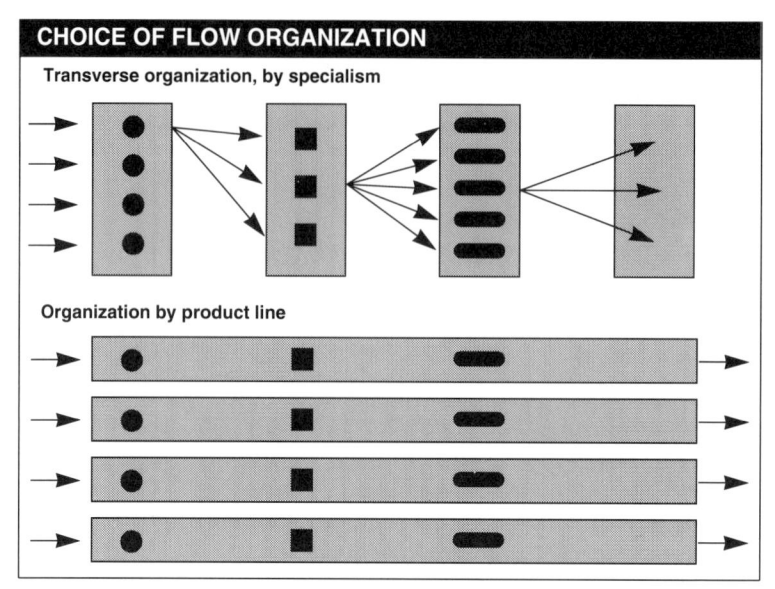

Organization by product line

**FIGURE 25**            **PARALLELIZATION**

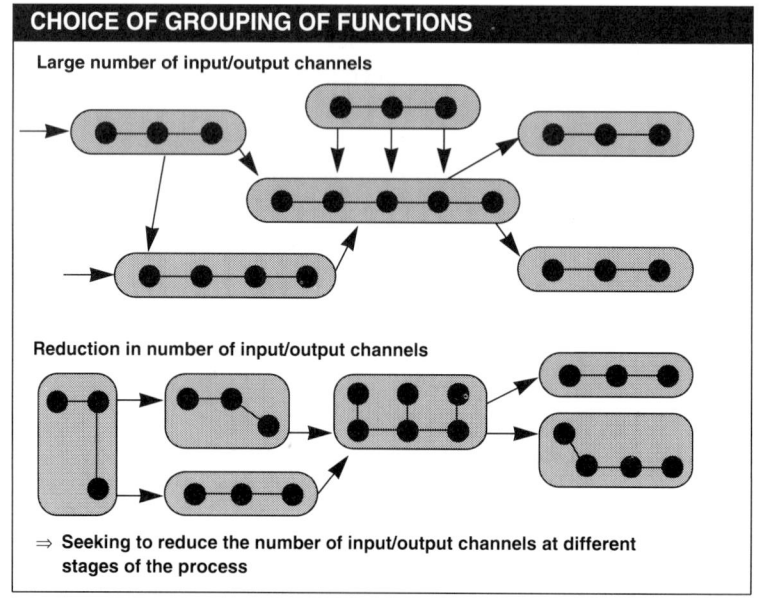

**CHOICE OF GROUPING OF FUNCTIONS**

Large number of input/output channels

Reduction in number of input/output channels

⇒ Seeking to reduce the number of input/output channels at different stages of the process

**FIGURE 26**            **SEGMENTATION**

94

## Establishing the organizational chart and hierarchical functions or the functions of managerial staff

This issue, which is closely linked to the question of information and management systems, must also be looked at separately.

The length of communications systems will depend on the *number of hierarchical levels*.

The role of the hierarchy and the style of management will depend largely on the *structure (of the production line and of management)*.

The trend is to establish organizational charts with fewer (three or four) hierarchical levels and to replace the lower levels of management with support teams of specialists or technicians. This runs parallel with the creation of autonomous work teams which are capable of analysing their own performance in relation to their objectives.

## Management and information systems

The construction of an organization involves fundamental choices as regards *management and information systems*: how, and in what form, is information to be gathered, assembled, processed and redistributed to facilitate guidance and decision-making?

Should information be available to work teams themselves so that they can monitor their performance and regulate it in real time? Or should information merely be used as a means of control, after the event, by other people and at other levels?

The reliability of information systems will largely depend on their usefulness for those on the shopfloor who generate the information and take immediate decisions.

### Skill and pay systems
Skill and pay systems are an integral part of the socio-technical design of an organization.

The skills required and actually used by workers must be identified and assessed.

How are roles and occupations defined? What coherent groupings do they form? What is the relation between the various occupations and skills and how do they affect career development? Is there sufficient recognition of training and improvement?

Are pay systems coherent and do they reinforce the logic according to which the organization functions?

### Methods by which the organization maintains and regulates its functioning and development
An organization must function as a living organism. Any effective organization must have methods of regulating its own functioning (meetings, channels of arbitration and appeal) and ensuring its own development (regular reassessment, evaluations, training, motivation exercises). It must be able to evolve and maintain constant potential for development if it is to be flexible enough to deal with unforeseen and unforeseeable changes.

---

REFERENCES
1 In "Modern Sociotechnology", Koers Consultants, 1989, Den Bosch, The Netherlands, 1989, p 18
2 See Friso den Hertog and L Ulbo de Sitter, "Integrated Organisational Design: a structural and strategic framework", Merit/NKWO-Koers, 1988

THE FACTORY OF THE FUTURE
SOCIO-TECHNICAL INVESTMENT MANAGEMENT
— EUROPEAN METHODS

PART ELEVEN

THE INTEGRATION OF FORWARD MANAGEMENT OF WORK AND TRAINING IN THE DESIGN PROCESS

Investment, especially if it is to lead to major technological advances within the company or the subsequent development of jobs and organization, must be accompanied by *planning of the human resources* concerned (directly and indirectly) and of the corresponding *training*.

## Forward management of work and qualifications

Forward management of work and qualifications lies in adjusting the work-force and skills to technical investment not after the event and as a consequence, but *simultaneously, as one of the parameters for optimizing choices*.

This means that the *characteristics of the work-force* — age, health, skills, level of training, development potential — must be taken into account and integrated into simulations in all the hypotheses and alternatives which have been formulated.

The three points of application of this process during investment are:

☐ the predicted evolution of JOBS,

☐ the adaptation of CLASSIFICATIONS,

☐ the study of occupational STREAMS.

The results in terms of action relate either to a progressive policy of *recruitment or redundancy* (or external redeployment) or to *training* (which will be discussed below).

### Evolution of jobs

Investment often entails far-reaching evolution of *jobs*, especially if it is part of a wider framework of organizational change. An approach through "jobs" is more than a simple analysis of tasks and associated technical expertise. It is the *overall job* which is in question:

> ☐ it includes the *professional or technical expertise*;
>
> ☐ as well as expertise as regards *organization, management* and *communication*;
>
> ☐ and in some cases an enrichment of the basic job so that it becomes a job which includes a minimum of *maintenance* and a proportion of *quality management/control*.

This evolution of jobs is often only germinal in the investment: it is important to project two or three years forward to target the new configurations of jobs and deduce what action needs to be taken over time. Forward management means *working out the time-scale* for these evolutions, anticipating them and managing them.

**Adjusting classifications**
Classification systems show the respective weight of tasks in grids which classify and position them in relation to one another and make it possible to agree on pay scales. Job changes throw these grids into confusion. Investment often has to be accompanied by a negotiated redesigning of these job classifications.

Since they are often reassessed upwards as a result of the investment, this provides an opportunity to introduce stricter controls into skill evaluations (as regards their acquisition and exercise). If this qualification management system is not reviewed or is reviewed at too late a stage, technical modernizations lead to labour conflicts brought about by the feeling that the new jobs and the new requirements of tasks have not been recognized.

### Professional streams and career developments

The new jobs carried on as part of flatter hierarchical structures offer less chance of development through the hierarchy. It is consequently important to map out genuine workers' careers, allowing professional development over 15 or 20 years, which are in keeping with the work-force's potential. An organization can be designed only in respect of its developments in the medium and long term.

## Integration of training in a socio-technical project

Formulating the desired skill profiles at a very early stage makes it possible to deduce the training strategies needed.

### An integrated-training approach

Three points should be emphasized if training is to be truly integrated in the process of joint design:

> ☐ *Training programmes must be based on a coherent organizational project*, which is defined at the same time as the technical project and is used to deduce the impact on employment, skills and job profiles.

> ☐ *Training must be programmed around the different stages of the technical project*, making use of all the training opportunities they afford. From this point of view, our comments on participation are of vital importance, and participation and training should not be seen as separate issues: participation is both the best form of training for future users and a prerequisite for further training.

> ☐ *Training must be planned* and must be taken into account at a very early stage of the project, in the preliminary studies. The reaction time of the human system is much

slower than that of technical systems. "Advance work" is therefore needed.

An example of the method used by a German *car manufacturer* can be seen on pp 102 and 103.

The first diagram shows the various periods scheduled for consideration of investments and of their impact in terms of training requirements.

The second diagram shows the interconnection of the various phases at both the design and implementation stage.

## The project itself as a training process

When speaking of training, people often think automatically of *unskilled workers* who "need training". In our view, a major industrial project tends, however, to lead to much more wide-ranging training needs because it heralds a whole new organizational culture for every member of the enterprise.

This new organizational culture includes relational as well as technical components, and these non-technical components cannot be learned in classes or from books. They are lessons that inform, and so can be learned from, the project itself: other methods of working, of managing, of communicating, of collaborating and co-operating.

It seems to us vital that this form of apprenticeship is considered for all members of the organization. The project itself, at the planning stage and on start-up, is the best possible apprenticeship for these new forms of collaboration and co-operation. It has to be planned and managed. This is "training" in the socio-technical sense.

## The training of managers and staff integrated in the PERT of the project

If the recruitment and training of staff and managers are

# THE FACTORY OF THE FUTURE

**Determination of continuing-training needs linked to investment**

| CONDUCT OF PLANNING | CONTENT OF PLANNING |
|---|---|
| Submission of investment programme | Overall redeployment needs |
| **1. Investment analysis** [1] | – number of workers<br>– nature of measures |
| Planning term: medium-term (2-3 years prior to implementation of programme) | |
| | Continuation |
| **2. Budget planning** [2] | Budgeting for continuing-training needs<br>– number of workers<br>– specification of continuing-training needs<br>– hours/participants |
| Determination of investment project needs which are already known | |
| Annual continuing-training programme (autumn of the preceding year) | |
| | Continuation |
| **3. Demonstration for authorization of project** [3] | Actual contunuing-training needs in comparison with plans |
| Economic evaluation of numbers using "checklist"<br>Planning of project personnel (8-4 months prior to the launch of the project) | – number of workers<br>– actual volumes<br>– training costs |

**FIGURE 27**

# THE INTEGRATION OF FORWARD MANAGEMENT

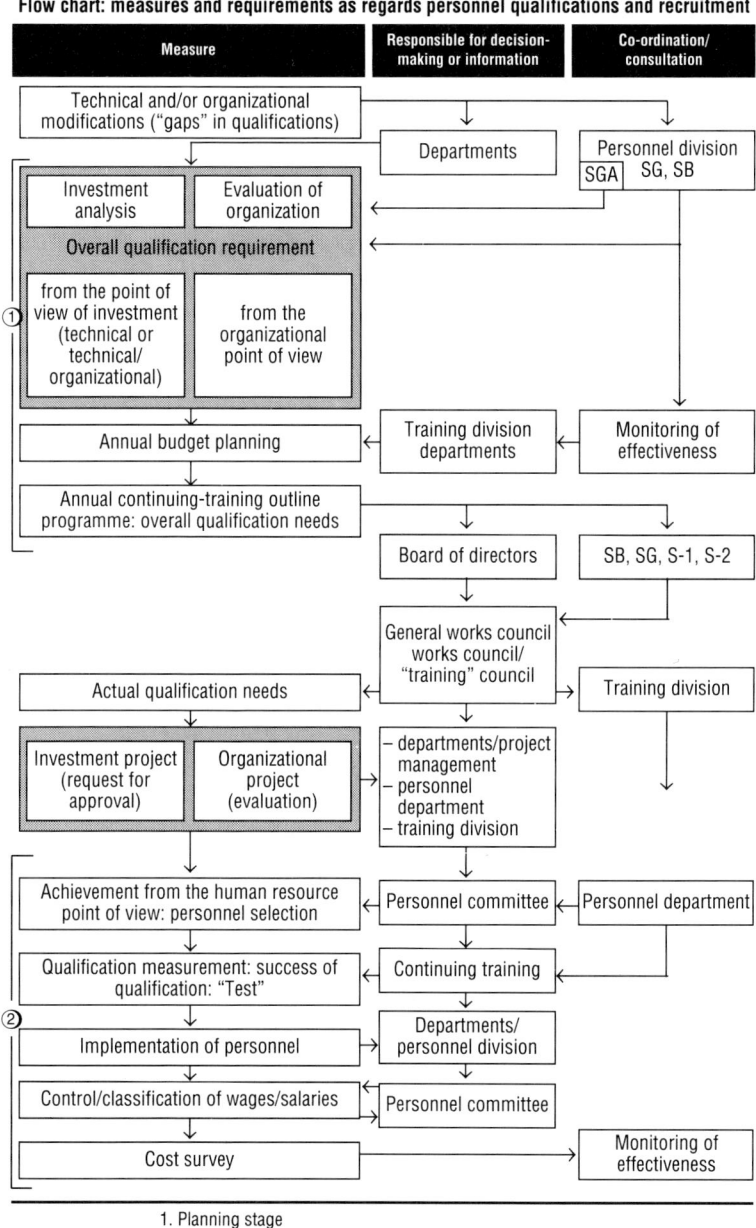

**Flow chart: measures and requirements as regards personnel qualifications and recruitment**

| Measure | Responsible for decision-making or information | Co-ordination/consultation |
|---|---|---|

Technical and/or organizational modifications ("gaps" in qualifications)
→ Departments
→ Personnel division / SGA / SG, SB

① 
- Investment analysis
- Evaluation of organization
- Overall qualification requirement
  - from the point of view of investment (technical or technical/organizational)
  - from the organizational point of view

Annual budget planning ← Training division departments ← Monitoring of effectiveness

Annual continuing-training outline programme: overall qualification needs

Board of directors — SB, SG, S-1, S-2

General works council works council/"training" council

Actual qualification needs → Training division

- Investment project (request for approval)
- Organizational project (evaluation)
→ departments/project management / personnel department / training division

Achievement from the human resource point of view: personnel selection ← Personnel committee ← Personnel department

Qualification measurement: success of qualification: "Test" ← Continuing training

② Implementation of personnel → Departments/personnel division

Control/classification of wages/salaries → Personnel committee

Cost survey → Monitoring of effectiveness

1. Planning stage
2. Implementation stage

**FIGURE 28**

not integrated in the project schedule, they will be out of line with the project and risk being neglected or completely ignored. Personnel development is the area which requires the most time and which should therefore be treated as a vital starting-point.

Failing this, the human factor will be sacrificed simply because it is the most flexible. Enterprises often seek to cut training time to make up for delays in the project.

## Training: an integral part of design

**1. INTEGRATED TRAINING**
- based on an organizational project
- included in each phase of the project
- provided for at a very early stage in the project

**2. THE PROJECT AS A TRAINING PROCESS**

**3. TRAINING INCLUDED IN THE PERT OF THE PROJECT**

**FIGURE 29**

## The Factory of the Future
Socio-technical Investment Management
— European Methods

## Part Twelve

## The Financial Viability of a Socio-technical Approach to Investment

The socio-technical approach to investment will not, whatever its virtues in terms of social relations or the improvement of working conditions, win acceptance unless we can also argue and prove that it guarantees a higher return on investment.

This issue covers four different but associated questions:

- that of the *soundness of the financial decision to invest*;
- that of the relationship between the *cost and quality of the design process itself*;
- that of *performance on start-up*;
- that of the *socio-productive performance of the plant* at the change-over stage.

These four points of concern in management thinking enrich a traditional approach to the study of the financial viability of an investment.

"Study of the viability of an investment consists of weighing capital expenditure against the income it will generate, which is the return on the investment. In the case of an industrial investment (risk capital), this return on investment must be guaranteed on two counts:

☐ sales, by the assurance of a *market* and a *profit margin* on sales;

☐ production, by the assurance of being able to contain *investment levels* (without overspending) and maintain *output*.

Our project-enrichment approach can strengthen the guarantees as regards production."[1]

The initial financial impact of the socio-technical approach is that it makes it possible to confirm the reliability of the socio-productive performances laid down at the outset as a basis for profitability of the investment, not only on start-up but also during the change-over phase.

Also, because it sets up a more efficient communications system, the socio-technical approach can guarantee speedier design and cheaper repetitions.

Thus the approach confirms the soundness of the financial decision, by an improved anticipation of effects and risks which makes it possible to consider appropriate responses at an earlier stage, ie when the investment decision is taken.

## Confirming the soundness of the decision to invest

An "enriched profitability study" is a study that:

- ☐ is based on a fuller and closer analysis of reference situations;
- ☐ integrates the performance or risk factor associated with the work-force and with the functioning of the social system.

In doing this, it makes it possible to identify more precisely the global (socio-technical) approach that will guarantee achievement of the desired performance levels, and to assess more accurately the level of investment required.

Profitability studies and financial investment reports usually have the shortcomings which we list on p 108 here to compare them with the advantages of an enriched profitability study.

## Cost/quality performance of design and implementation

The cost of the study must also be reduced by a better-quality project. How this can be achieved is outlined on pp 109-110.

# THE FACTORY OF THE FUTURE

| FAILINGS OF A TRADITIONAL PROFITABILITY STUDY | ADVANTAGES OF AN ENRICHED PROFITABILITY STUDY |
|---|---|
| Places too much stress on the productivity of the work-force | The productivity factors taken into account cover a broader area:<br>– quality<br>– consumption<br>– stocks and work in progress<br>– flexibility<br>– period of use<br>– productivity structure, etc |
| Ill-supported hypotheses on future functioning ratios | A closer study of problems makes estimates of ratios more reliable.<br>People who are to be responsible for those ratios participate in the studies |
| Poor assessment of risks (start-up problems, social problems, etc) | Risks anticipated and responses identified in advance |
| Intangible aspects of the investment underestimated: training, organization, participation, etc | Training and preparation of the organization defined at the same time as the capital investment |
| Supplements associated with conditions of use are often necessary | These aspects are included in the investment package |
| Costly corrections must be made at a later date | Responsibility of suppliers increased by more stringent specifications |

**FIGURE 30**

**Doing things properly from the start**
The study phase of a project becomes expensive when studies have to be reconducted because of a failure to include certain information or to consult certain actors, holders of information or pertinent viewpoints in due time. This is expensive in terms of the time spent on additional studies and the delays this causes in the project.

The principle of socio-technical project management is to set up and operate a complicated communications system which links the key actors on the operational side from the moment studies begin.

We know of projects in one factory which the research firm had to start from scratch three times because it had not consulted users on the feasibility of the projects from the operational point of view at a sufficiently early stage.

The socio-technical approach usually takes a little longer in the beginning, because more time is spent on defining problems and objectives and because of the broader concertation involved. But this time is largely made up during the detailed project phase and implementation. A less linear and less hierarchical structure, capable of rapid adjustment and broken down into informal working groups, ensures that the information available is very "rich" and that tasks can be performed quickly.

**Additional work equals additional cost**
Corrections and additions after ordering or after start-up are even more expensive than having to begin studies afresh. Enriched project management can lead to savings in that all the constraints that need to be introduced are integrated in the invitation to tender sent to suppliers. If outside suppliers are not invited to tender, all the desired effects or performances in terms of quality are integrated in the design itself.

Any request for corrections or qualitative improvements after ordering or after implementation will be very expensive.

Everyone is aware, for example, of the exorbitant cost of sound-proofing when it is installed to correct a problem; but it can often be integrated in the design at no extra cost or with the minimum of expense. Sound-proofing measures are, then, structurally integrated in the technical project: noisy pumps are isolated, sources of vibration are rendered more flexible (floating floors, insulation sheaths for piping systems, etc).

## Start-up: the moment of truth and a key factor in profitability

The point when all is revealed in a well-managed project is the moment of start-up. And it is also the moment of greatest risk: the risk of delayed improvement in performance, risks associated with the work-force's inability to adjust, risks of social conflict, risks concerning the quality achieved, etc.

Good management of the investment during the study and implementation stages makes it possible to achieve expected performance levels or to react quickly to any shortfalls noted because, in particular, the work-force has been prepared by participation and training.

By contrast, a few weeks or even a few months of problems, adjustments and failure to achieve the required quality can lead to the loss of markets and may threaten the profitability of the investment.

## Operation

Finally, by assessing production ratios (labour per tonne produced, rejects, alterations, delays, consumption, actual operation time, etc) during a period of stable production, it is possible to evaluate the success of the project and its real profitability. The envisaged return on the investment is also calculated by anticipating these ratios.

This "looping", which will from project to project give credence to profitability calculations, assumes that these project evaluations are in fact conducted (see Part Thirteen, Project evaluation).

Here too, as in the case of start-up, desired performance levels will be reached:

- ☐ if the intangible investment (organization, training, etc) has not been underestimated;

- ☐ if the work-force has participated and been prepared;

- ☐ if account has been taken of the experience of "producers" in the design of plants.

If we were asked to summarize in a few words what it is that makes the socio-technical approach advantageous in a design process, we should do so by contrasting, somewhat simplistically, the two existing approaches:

- ☐ The instinctive tendency of design engineers is as far as possible to eliminate the work-force factor because it is, for them, the most uncertain and unreliable one (hence the excessive emphasis on work-force productivity). The result of this is that the "spurned" factor takes its revenge in practice and often threatens the success of the project.

- ☐ In the socio-technical approach, the human factor is taken into account, drawn in and seen as a key factor of success. This is the source of the difference in profitability of the two approaches.

# THE FACTORY OF THE FUTURE

**This is the analysis grid presented in "Réussir l'investissement productif" (Successful investment in production), p 133, as a path to the achievement of objectives:**

| Objectives or performance ratios set | Risks or elements at stake as regards profitability of the investment | Problems or risks considered in the enrichment study | Measures taken in the project to guarantee achievement of objectives ||||| Associated cost |
|---|---|---|---|---|---|---|---|---|
| | | | Studies | Training | Additional investment | Suppliers' guarantees | Other measures | |
| 1 Quality<br>2 Period of use of equipment<br>3 Flexibility<br>4 Work-force productivity<br>5 Materials and energy productivity<br>6 Maintenance conditions | | | | | | | | |
| 7 Health and safety, social facilities<br>8 Physical environment<br>9 Workload<br>10 Job content and job satisfaction<br>11 Communication and co-operation<br>12 Advancement and training | | | | | | | | |
| 13 Work-force structure and skills<br>14 Hierarchy and organization chart<br>15 Information and management system<br>16 Interdepartmental relations<br>17 Flows, traffic, stocks<br>18 Links with the environment | | | | | | | | |
| 19 to 24 } Developments<br>Start-up | | | | | | | | |

**FIGURE 31**

## An essential prerequisite: a management system that spots "hidden costs"

There is, however, an essential prerequisite to all this financial assessment of a socio-technical approach to investment management. Enterprises' management systems are very often ill-equipped to identify a number of costs which could be cut by taking a socio-technical approach.

Over the years, methods have been developed to calculate *"hidden costs"*. These are the costs of dysfunctions in socio-productive systems, identified at a level (workshops or sub-systems) that makes it possible to trace them to identifiable causes.

This process, which was first used in the late 1970s in France[2] and in the Federal Republic of Germany,[3] has returned to the fore in "total quality" methods, in the form of "costs of non-quality".

### Financial viability of a socio-technical approach to investment

1. Confirming the decision to invest

2. Performance of the design process:
   – doing things properly from the start
   – additional work equals additional cost

3. Start-up: the key factor of profitability

4. Operation and assessment

Essential prerequisite: the calculation of hidden costs

FIGURE 32

It is therefore important, when analysing problems concerning operation and working conditions that need to be solved as part of an investment project, to be able to discuss in financial terms the cost of the dysfunctions identified and the potential financial gain in correcting them.

---

REFERENCES

1. O du Roy *et al*, "Réussir l'investissement productif", Paris, Editions d'Organisation, 1985, p 128
2. See "Le coût des conditions de travail" (The cost of working conditions), Paris, ANACT, 1979, and the works of H Savall, eg "Maîtriser les coûts cachés" (Controlling hidden costs), Paris, Economica, 1987
3. "Die Kosten der Arbeitsbedingungen", translated into German by G Schoenberg, EIFIP, Frankfurt, October 1982; and also various research works on the same subject conducted by the RKW under its programme "Humanisierung des Arbeitslebens" (Humanization of working life): "Menschengerechte Arbeitsplätze sind wirtschaftlich" (Workplaces suitable for people are economic), 1985

# THE FACTORY OF THE FUTURE
## SOCIO-TECHNICAL INVESTMENT MANAGEMENT
## — EUROPEAN METHODS

# PART THIRTEEN

# PROJECT EVALUATION

Any learning process implies the setting-up of a system of assessment that makes it possible to gain from experience and to transform even mistakes into a source of progress. It is essential to bring this process to bear in project management if we are to develop the skills associated with the socio-technical approach.

Project evaluation must be conducted as far as possible by the project team, in collaboration with those who have participated, whether closely or indirectly, in implementing the project in question. Evaluation consists of two processes:

- ☐ assessment of the project as a functioning industrial system;
- ☐ analysis of the process of project management, which may explain the end result and may give rise to improvements in that process.

## Assessment of the investment in operation

**Analysis of the performance of the investment**
From the point of view of production, quality and cost.

From the point of view of the satisfaction of workers and management (of the various departments).

From the point of view of working conditions.

**Analysis of the completed project**
How it meets expectations.

Length of project from start to finish.

Compliance with budget.

**Outstanding problems raised by users**
Inadequacies or flaws pointed out by production, maintenance, quality-control workers, etc.

## Analysis of the process of investment management

### Decision
Source of the original idea (genesis of the project).

Grounds for, and preparation of, the decision to invest.

### Negotiation
Were the social partners kept informed, and included in negotiations?

At what stages in the project?

On what topics?

Joint working groups.

### Phases
The constituent stages or phases of the project (post-project reconstruction).

Planning, announcement and respect of the various phases (pre-project planning).

### Project team, roles and participation
Project leader (contracting enterprise's side).

Project leader (contractor's side).

Members of the project team.

Involvement of future users (cf Figure 17, p 45).

Participation of management and workers.

Frequency of project meetings.

### Consideration of known problems in the existing situation
Investigation and consideration of known problems in existing situations.

Interviews, studies and meetings in this connection.

**Objectives of the project**
The industrial and social objectives of the project.

Announcement of those objectives.

When and by whom those objectives were defined.

Involvement of the project team in the definition of objectives.

The "enrichment" of objectives on the basis of the enterprise's own objectives.

**Alternatives**
The identification of alternatives and their presentation to the decision-maker.

Presentation of facts and figures concerning alternatives (including information regarding margins for error).

**Dealings with suppliers**
Invitation to tender.

Involvement of suppliers as "partners" in the project.

Assessment of suppliers.

Invitations to tender based on ("enriched") specifications.

Analysis of tenders.

Decision-making criteria and the person(s) responsible for decision-making.

Monitoring of suppliers' work and the person(s) responsible for monitoring.

**Site work**
Unsolved problems on site.

Site work and assembly work by suppliers as part of the training process.

Persons involved in site work.

## Training

Definition and implementation of training (timing).

Training budget in relation to total project budget.

External training services (invitation to tender?).

Training provided in-house.

Suppliers' contribution to training.

Assessment of training (follow-up, practical application).

Completion of training in due time.

Technical supports for training (drawings, diagrams, operating instructions, etc) (available at appropriate time?).

Definition of areas covered by the "training budget" and areas covered by the "total project budget".

## Acceptance and start-up

"Authorization of delivery", provisional acceptance (including safety) and final acceptance; person(s) responsible for such authorization and acceptance.

Person(s) participating in acceptance and start-up.

"Handing-over" process.

Difficulties and delays.

Preparation for start-up.

Problems (reservations) on start-up.

Human resources involved in start-up and their suitability vis-à-vis the nature of the investment and the degree of innovation.

## Evaluation

When, how and by whom?

Adjustments and corrections.

"Learning from experience" — its recording for use in future projects.

# The Factory of the Future
## Socio-technical Investment Management
## — European Methods

# Conclusion

In a 1984 publication on the design of work in automated production systems, F Butera[1] laid down five basic recommendations for socio-technical design. This remarkable text provides an excellent summary of the content of this report:

## Five recommendations for socio-technical design

- "goal and problem setting in an analytical, explicit, concrete way, including social goals and problems as well as technical ones;

- formal steps for finding design alternatives for the organization and social system. It is proposed that this be done when secondary technology is designed. A well thought-out interaction procedure with the process of technical design is also recommended;

- training of engineers as well as social specialists to see both the human and the technical sides of the socio-technical systems and possibly to use socio-technical methodologies of analysis and design;

- responsibility for design assigned to a temporary unit including managers and technicians from different functional areas, as well as knowledgeable manual and technical workers who are to be involved in operating the new system. In addition, appropriate ways need to be found of informing the trade union and, in some cases, assuring its participation in the various steps; and

- sanction from top management and the design of an interactive procedure for decision-making."

# CONCLUSION

In a context of heightened international competition, the optimization of investment has become a condition of survival. There is no longer any margin for error, which means that social and technical issues must be considered simultaneously. Right from the very beginning of an investment project, it is essential that careful thought be given to organizational choices, occupational skills, ergonomics and plant management.

The question is how to proceed, how to reverse the logic according to which most enterprises give priority to technical issues and the last word to the engineer? This is the question we have attempted to answer in this booklet by outlining a possible methodology, with examples drawn from the approaches taken by a number of enterprises in the European Community.

REFERENCES

1   In F Butera and J Thurman, "Automation and Work Design", North Holland, 1984, p 68

# The Factory of the Future
Socio-technical Investment Management
— European Methods

# Bibliography

## 1. FRANCE AND BELGIUM

F. DANIELLOU
L'opérateur, la vanne, l'écran, l'ergonomie des salles de contrôle, (The operator, the valve, the screen, the ergonomics of control rooms), ANACT, Paris, 1986; course on ergonomics and industrial projects, CNAM, 1988-1989.

F. DECOSTER
Vers une démarche socio-technique en productique, (Towards a socio-technical approach to production technology), ANACT, Paris, 1989.

O. du ROY, J-C. HUNAULT, J. TUBIANA
Réussir l'investissement productif (Successful investment in production), Editions d'Organisation, Paris, 1985.

O. du ROY et J. TUBIANA
Le rôle des exploitants dans l'investissement industriel. De la conception à la mise en exploitation des projets, (The role of operators in industrial investment. Projects from idea to start-up), in Techniques de l'Ingénieur, A-8500, 1987.

FUC-CFDT
Négocier les changements du travail, (Negotiating changes in work), Editions INPACT, Paris, 1989.

J. LAPLACE et D. REGNAUD
Démarche participative et investissement technique, la méthodologie de Rhône-Poulenc, (The participative approach and technical investment — the method applied by Rhône-Poulenc), Cahiers Techniques de l'UIMM, No. 52, 1986.

F. MAIRE et J-M. BRUMENT
Conduite de projet industriel. Pour une coopération ingénierie-exploitation, (Industrial-project management. For co-operation between engineers and operators), Editions d'organisation and ANACT, Paris, 1988.

## 2. UNITED KINGDOM

A. CHERNS
Principles of sociotechnical design revisited, in Human Relations, 40, 1987, pp. 153-162.

P.G. HERBST
Socio-technical design: strategies in multidisciplinary research, Tavistock Publication, London, 1974.

F.E. EMERY
Characteristics of sociotechnical systems, Tavistock Publication, London, 1959.

A.K. RICE
Productivity and social organisation, Tavistock Publication, London, 1958.

3. USA

L.E. DAVIS
Organisation Design, in G. Salvendy, Handbook of Industrial Engineering, John Wiley, NY, 1982.

L.E. DAVIS
Joint Design of organisations and advanced technology in manufacturing: the quality of working life and the future of plant engineering, paper for the RSO international conference on "Joint design of technology, organization and people growth", Venice, October 1988.

4. ITALY

F. BUTERA
La divisione del lavoro in fabbrica, (The division of labour in the factory), Marsilie Editore, Venice, 1977.

F. BUTERA
Lavoro umano e prodotto tecnico. (Human labour and the technical product), a study of the Terni steelworks, G. Einaudi, Turin, 1979.

F. BUTERA and J. THURMAN
Automation and work design, ILO, Geneve, 1982; North Holland, 1984.

F. BUTERA
Information technology, new patterns of organisation, emerging professional paths in the network enterprise, paper for the RSO international conference on "Joint design of technology, organisation and people growth," Venice, October 1988.

5. GERMANY

ADAMCZYK, GARTNER, LEDERER, SANDER
Arbeitsstrukturierung: Planungssystematik mit Entscheidungs- und Handlungshilfen, (Structuring of work: planning system with aids

to decision-making and action), AEG-Telefunken, central department of production and working techniques, Frankfurt, February 1980.

H.J. ELIAS
**Gestaltung und Bewertung von Arbeitssystemen**, (Creation and assessment of work systems), Campus Verlag, Frankfurt/Main, New York, 1985.

E. FRICKE
**Qualifikation und Beteiligung: das "Peiner Modell"**, (Qualifications and participation: the "Peiner model"), Friedrich-Ebert-Stiftung research institute, Humanisierung des Arbeitslebens (Humanization of working life) series, Vol 12, Campus Verlag, Frankfurt/Main, New York, 1981.

R. GROB
**Planungsleitlinien Arbeitsstrukturierung : Systematik zur Gestaltung von Arbeitssystemen** (Planning guidelines for the structuring of work: a system of creating work systems), Siemens A.G. (publications department), Berlin, Munich, 1982.

H. RIECKMANN
**Auf der grünen Wiese..., Organisationsentwicklung en Werksneugründung, soziotechn. Design und offene Systemplanung** (Greenfield sites..., organization development and setting-up of new plant, socio-technical design and open system planning), Organisationsentwicklung in der Praxis, 3, Haupt, Berne, Stuttgart, 1982.

B. SIEVERS
**Werksneugründungen als organisationsentwickung: Soziotechnisches Design und Partizipation bei Fabrikplanungen,** (Setting-up of new plant as organization development: socio-technical design and participation in factory planning), Zeitschrift für Organisation, 1, 1983, pp 67-79.

V.D.I.
**Handlungsempfehlung: "Sozialverträgliche Gestaltung von Automatisierungsvorhaben"**, (Recommendation for action: "Shaping automation projects via social compacts"), VDI, Düsseldorf, 1989.

P. BROEDNER
**Fabrik 2000. Alternative Entwicklungspfade in die Zukunft der Fabrik,** (Factory 2000. Alternative development routes to the factory of the future), Sigma Bohn, Berlin, 1985.

6. **THE NETHERLANDS**

   J-T. ALLEGRO
   Sociotechnische organisatie-ontwikkeling (Socio-technical organization development), Stenfest Kroese, Leiden, 1973.

   M.J.J. van BEINUM, M. GILS, E.J. VERHAGEN
   Taakontwerp en werkorganisatie in een sociotechnisch veldexperiment, (Job design and work organization in a sociotechnical field experiment), NIPG, Leiden, 1967.

   J.J. BOONSTRA, M.I. DEMENINT, H.O. STEENSMA
   Organiseren en veranderen in een dynamische wereld, begeleiden van verangeringsprocessen binnen organisaties (Organization and change in a dynamic world, accompanied by processes of change within organizations), Lemma, Culemborg, 1989.

   A.A.F. BROUWER, F. VAAS, F.D. POT
   Sociaal Inventief Automatiseren, Integratie van arbeid en Techniek in de Ontwerpfase, (Socially inventive automation, integration of work and technology in the design phase), FNV Steunpunt Technologie, Amsterdam, 1987.

   J. FRISO DEN HERTOG et L. ULBO de SITTER
   Integrated Organisational Design: a structural and strategic framework, paper for the RSO international conference on "Joint design of technology, organisation and people growth", Venice, October 1988; Merit/NKVO-Koers, Maastricht, 1988.

   L. ULBO de SITTER
   Modern sociotechnology, Koers Consultants, Den Bosch, 1989.

7. **SWEDEN**

   S. AGUREN, J. EDGREN
   Des Usines différentes, pour une nouvelle théorie des systèmes de production, (Different factories, for a new production-systems theory), SAF, Stockholm, 1975, French translation ANACT, Paris, 1981.

   P. ENTSTROM, B. GUSTAVSEN
   Worker participation and new Principles for the design of factories, the case Volvo, in Productivity and the Future of Work, Munich, 1986; RKW, Eschborn, 1987.

European Communities — Commission

The Factory of the Future: Socio-technical investment management

Luxembourg: Office for Official Publications of the European Communities

1992 — 130 pp. — 210 x 148 mm

ISBN 92-826-3529-5

Catalogue number: SY-72-91-980-EN-C

Price (excluding VAT) in Luxembourg: ECU 11.25